Day Trading
Grain Futures

Every owner of a physical copy of this edition of

Day Trading Grain Futures

can download the eBook for free direct from us at Harriman House, in a DRM-free format that can be read on any eReader, tablet or smartphone.

Simply head to:

ebooks.harriman-house.com/daytradinggrain2nd

to get your copy now.

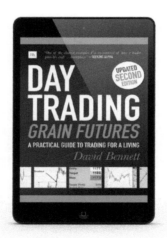

Day Trading Grain Futures

A practical guide to trading for a living

SECOND EDITION

David Bennett

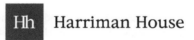 Harriman House

HARRIMAN HOUSE LTD
18 College Street
Petersfield
Hampshire
GU31 4AD
GREAT BRITAIN
Tel: +44 (0)1730 233870

Email: enquiries@harriman-house.com
Website: www.harriman-house.com

First published in Great Britain in 2009. This second edition published in 2017.
Copyright © David Bennett

The right of David Bennett to be identified as the author has been asserted in accordance with the
Copyright, Design and Patents Act 1988.

Paperback ISBN: 978-0-85719-659-0
eBook ISBN: 978-0-85719-660-6

British Library Cataloguing in Publication Data
A CIP catalogue record for this book can be obtained from the British Library.

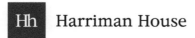 Harriman House

CONTENTS

ABOUT THE AUTHOR

DAVID BENNETT is a futures trader living on the Gold Coast in Australia. His formal career spanned computing, teaching and human resource management, but his passion is trading. "For many years I tried every trading technique I heard about, with indifferent results, but then I got into day trading grain futures – and I've never looked back!" A citizen of three countries, UK, New Zealand and Australia, David has followed the sun. "The trouble is my body keeps adapting, and I have to go somewhere warmer!" However, a youngster at school means staying put, for now at least. David initially became interested in finance and trading when he was chairman of the trustees of a large superannuation fund, working closely with professional fund managers. He believes that a fit body sharpens the mind, and tries to spend as much time as possible jogging, surfing or hitting a ball on the squash court. He has served as a Community Magistrate in New Zealand.

David's recent focus has been on developing commercial-grade software to fully automate his personal trading. "This project saved me a huge amount of time and stress, while improving my trading accuracy. My idea was to turn my PC into a money machine working in the spare room while I went surfing!" He markets this software at **TradeOnAuto.com.**

A NOTE ON THE
Second Edition

IT'S BEEN NEARLY ten years since I wrote the first edition of this book, and things change. But, of course, the more things change, the more they stay the same…

When I wrote the first edition, I traded manually. I was a night owl, because Chicago markets open around midnight here in Australia. I used the method described in this book, and it was an adrenaline-pumping experience. But late nights and broken sleep weren't quite the ideal I was aiming for. Really, I wanted my PC to be a money machine, whirring away in the spare room, while I got on with a busy retirement.

Fortunately, I was educated in computer science. So, after the book was published, I dusted off dormant programming skills and began automating my trading. Eventually, I built a software tool (called TradeOnAUTO) that enabled me to start my program early in the day and leave it trading, automatically while I slept. This was a huge step forward; I gained good quality sleep, saved several hours per day, and my strategy was always executed flawlessly (no mistakes!).

In 2013, the CME (Chicago Mercantile Exchange), bless them, twice changed the trading hours of the grains complex. This changed the trading characteristics of those markets, resulting in a poor period for my strategy, and forced me to look at other markets. I developed a simulator, feeding old market sessions into my program to see how various strategy permutations would perform over time. I liked this approach so much that I built it into TradeOnAUTO, so I could easily research new strategies. Now, as well as grains, I trade S&P 500 E-mini futures and the energy complex (oil, heating oil, petroleum).

So, yes, much has changed, but the technique is still the same, with a few minor tweaks here and there. The parameters in other markets differ from those used in the book – for example, I no longer focus my attention solely on two-minute candles. (Twenty-four-hour markets respond better to longer time frames.) It's perfectly feasible to trade this technique manually (just as I used to), and indeed for a beginner seeking to get the "feel" of market trading, I believe it's a good idea to do so. Practise with a paper trading account before using a live account – markets bite! Apart from changing a few factual items (such as those pesky trading hours!) I've left the text unaltered, because it captures the technique beautifully. I've added a few chapters at the end, random thoughts of an old trader…

David Bennett
2017

PREFACE

What this book covers

THIS BOOK IS about trading soybean, wheat and corn (the "grains") futures contracts. The contracts are traded at the CME in Chicago. Only the electronic contracts are considered because these can be traded efficiently by anybody with a reliable internet connection, no matter where they are located.

(Strictly speaking, soybeans are oilseeds, not grains. But rather than refer to the "grain and oilseeds complex", which is a bit of a mouthful, I just refer to the grains.)

While the book does not discuss options, CFDs, spread betting, or any other derivative products, much of its content is relevant to people trading those instruments. Indeed, I have worked with traders who successfully apply these techniques to trading ordinary shares. This methodology is not market specific.

The focus is on day trading (not holding the positions overnight), but that is purely my preference. There is nothing preventing these same techniques from being used to find and manage trades in other time frames.

In short, the book is all about how I day trade the grain markets. But the techniques employed are broadly applicable to most markets and time frames.

Some readers might wish for a broader description of trading techniques. There are, after all, an endless number of trading styles and systems out there. But this book was born out of a project to document exactly what I do, and why I do it, on a day-to-day basis as I trade the markets. It concentrates on the style I use, on the system choices I have made, and doesn't make any attempt to discuss alternatives.

Who this book is for

This book is written for people who have (probably) already done a bit of trading and are looking for a disciplined methodology that aims to earn reasonable returns while managing risk sensibly. The text will resonate well among those with prior experience in the markets, because its emphasis is on the realities of the trading process, not just theory.

That said, I have worked with clients who have never traded before. The book contains all the information needed to apply my methods, but it is not a trading textbook.

For example, my introduction to charting in chapter 8 is very brief. It tells you what you need to know to implement my trading approach, and no more. It makes no claim to be a comprehensive introduction to the subject.

As a further example, when I discuss order types, I talk exclusively about the order types I use to implement my approach, but I don't provide a description of all the order types available to traders. If I don't need it, I don't describe it.

A novice *can* use this book, and I think they would learn a lot from it. But he or she should be prepared to supplement the coverage here with further reading and research. The books recommended in the Appendix would be useful in this respect.

Every subject has its own jargon, and trading is no exception. I've generally tried to define the terms I use, but as my target audience is people with some trading experience, a complete newcomer may come across terms that puzzle them. Again, the recommended texts in the Appendix will help, or a simple search on the internet will generally bring enlightenment.

How the book is structured

When I go to the technical bookshop, I sit down with several trading books and browse through them. As often as not, I find a chapter or so in each book that interests me, and skip the rest. I've tried to make this into a book that *I* would like to read the whole way through.

I recognise that some chapters or sections may be skipped by more experienced readers. These chapters or sections have been left in because I wanted the book to be a complete description of my trading approach, and some very basic introduction to, for example, charts is necessary in this context, because charts are so fundamental to my approach.

Having said that, I've tried to be concise and keep most chapters short. Anything that isn't directly relevant to my method has been pruned from the text.

If I were reading this book, I'd probably read quickly through the earlier chapters, and slow down when I get to chapters 9–14, which really describe my trading approach. Then I would spend quite a bit of time studying the charts in chapters 15 and 16 to see how it all works in practice, and to check that I thoroughly understand the setups. I'd speed up again for the last three chapters.

However, I'm biased. I think nearly every chapter contains some nugget of worthwhile information that even the experienced trader will value – otherwise, I would have chopped it out!

Acknowledgment

I am grateful to Interactive Brokers for granting permission to reproduce charts plotted on their TWS software.

PROLOGUE

THE RINGING OF the alarm on my mobile jars me awake. It's
9:15 a.m.[1] in Chicago, 15 minutes after midnight here on the
Gold Coast in Queensland, Australia.

Show time!

I brew a pot of tea, log in to my broker, bring up my trading screens
and update the initial values in my spreadsheet.

Ready.

Dead on 00:30 the charts spring to life as the grain pits open at the
Chicago Board of Trade. Although some traders in bright coloured
jackets still shout raucously at each other in the trading pits, sealing
deals with weird hand signals, nowadays most trading is done
electronically. By people like me.

At 00:34 two candles have formed on my chart and I see an opportunity
for a short trade if the market breaks downwards. I place an entry order
with a single mouse click. Thirty seconds later the order is triggered
and I'm in the market! Short seven corn contracts. Two more quick
mouse clicks enter stop loss and profit-taking orders.

---

1   Since 2013, grain markets have opened an hour earlier.

At 00:42 the profit target is hit and my position closes. I've made 6 points per contract, 42 points in total. At $50 per point, that's $2100 in total profit, less about $45 brokerage.

I sip the rest of my tea and check out the news in the first editions of the morning papers on the internet. Then I confirm my little boy is sleeping soundly before slipping back into bed.

PART I:
Day Trading Grain Futures

CHAPTER 1:
Introduction

I MAKE A LIVING day trading grain futures.

It's a great life and I love it. Trading is not just my job; it's an addictive, absorbing hobby. Get it right, and it's the best job in the world.

This book tells you how to trade with good technique. There's no guarantee of riches, but the odds are with you if you do it well.

Trading for a living means I'm not interested in systems which are profitable in the long term, but subject to months, sometimes years, of losing periods. I want losing weeks to be rare and losing months virtually unheard of.

This is no general trading textbook. I focus on a specific trading niche, and how to exploit it. Nor does it contain chapters on trading psychology. All I will say on that subject is that it is one thing to have a trading plan, but quite another to have the willpower to stick to it.

There are many textbooks out there and if you study the literature you will quickly come across three important trading ideas:

1. support and resistance

2. the trend is your friend

3. it is best to let winners run and cut losses quickly.

This information normally comes in chapters 1 or 2 before authors get their teeth into the meaty topics of their books – be it sophisticated technical analysis, complex option techniques, arbitrage, seasonal spreads or whatever.

After all, trading is for smart people, right?

The good news is that these three very basic trading ideas, so frequently skipped over by the tyro seeking a silver bullet, contain the wisdom needed to trade fast-moving markets successfully.

Ideas are one thing. Turning them into a profitable day trading strategy is another matter, and it is the purpose of this book to show you how I do that.

CHAPTER 2:
Why Trade the Grains?

I AM OFTEN ASKED why I trade the grain contracts, as opposed to the popular stock index contracts, treasury bonds or currencies. The answer is that I find the grain contracts easier and more convenient to trade. On occasions, I will trade other commodities, but not often.

VOLATILITY

A day trader likes volatility, and the grains have more than enough to keep you happy. Without substantial price movement in each session, there is not enough scope for a day trader to make good profits. With the price per bushel moving anything from 20 to 60 cents in a session (sometimes much more), there is ample opportunity to profit when you consider that each cent the price changes translates to a $50 profit or loss on a futures contract.

Typically, corn has the least volatility, soybeans the highest volatility and wheat is somewhere in the middle. This is normally reflected in the margins. (Recent volatility in the wheat market made it more volatile than soybeans, with a higher margin, but this has not been the typical historical situation.)

VOLUME

Volatility is all very well, but you also need good volume. Otherwise, your trading is likely to be adversely affected by slippage. The front contracts in the grains all score very well in this respect. Typically, corn has the highest volumes, followed by soybeans, and wheat is third.

In most market situations, you get away with around a quarter point of slippage on stop orders, although recently it has been wise to allow half a point for wheat.

TRADING HOURS

I like to trade the open, when there is the greatest volume and big price swings. With twenty-four-hour trading in the index and currency contracts, there is no clear-cut open any more. The grains, however, have a distinct open at 08:30 (US Central Time). I consider this an enormous advantage for my type of trading. There are other traditional commodities with clear-cut opens, coffee and cotton for example, but they don't have the volumes you see in the grains.

Speaking of time, there is another advantage with the grains. The primary market session is less than five hours (08:30–13:20 US Central Time). Other contracts have longer primary sessions. I don't know about you, but I prefer a five-hour day to an eight-hour day!

CONTRACT TERMS

The three grain contracts I trade all have the same contract structure. A one cent price change (a *point*) is worth $50. The minimum move is a quarter point (a *pip*). This is the same as the very popular S&P

500 E-mini futures contract, so any trader familiar with that market would feel very comfortable with the grains.

Finally, and this is a subjective view, the grains seem a little easier to trade. The bond and index futures markets are very large and no doubt the institutions assign their best traders to them. The grains probably get the second tier.

Who would you rather trade against?

CHAPTER 3:
Why Day Trading?

WHEN I'M NOT being asked why I trade the grains, I'm being asked why I day trade. Especially as day trading comes in for quite a bit of criticism from some commentators and internet bloggers. Day trading is distinguished from other trading styles by the fact that all positions are closed at the end of the trading day.

INSTANT GRATIFICATION

I'm an impatient man. When I knock off from work, I like to know how I've done today. I don't want to wait days, weeks or months to see how a trade turns out! Last night I stalked my trade for about an hour, spent about five minutes in the trade, made over $1000 and went to bed.

REDUCED RISK

Futures are leveraged instruments. That's why I use them; for the opportunity of making large returns on modest capital investments. But I've traded for a long time, and one thing I've learned is that you want to minimise your time in the market with leveraged instruments, because they are risky.

Now, as a conservative day trader, I plan to take at most one trade per day, and no matter whether the trade is winning or losing, I close it before the end of the session. This means my money is at risk for the minimum amount of time. The rest of the time it is sitting in a safe money management account.

Consider the trade I took last night.

All up, my money was in the market for just over five minutes. While I was stalking the trade, *it was safe*. After I closed the trade, *it was safe*. While the market was closed, *it was safe*.

Market shocks occur more often than you would expect. Wars, natural disasters, terrorist attacks and government actions can all cause markets to react violently. As likely as not, they occur when the market is closed.

You never know what's coming in the markets. The worst loss I ever suffered was caused by a cow!

I had sold live cattle put options at a time when price was rising steadily. The position was winning about $18k, and I was basking in the warm glow of another successful trade. Then on Christmas Eve, 2003, somebody found a mad cow in the US. The contract price plummeted.

I was on holiday in New Zealand. I logged onto my account on Christmas morning and found the position was down over $280k.

Some Christmas present that was!

What's more, the market was locked session after session, and it was weeks before I could slink out of those positions and lick my wounds.

Don't assume that stop loss orders will protect you in this scenario. When the market goes mad, prices will bust right through those stops inflicting losses far greater than you allowed for. Believe me, the safest place is on the side-lines!

> **Now I plan my trades like surgical strikes; in and out of the market as fast as possible. And I never have an open leveraged position outside normal trading hours.**

STEADY PROFITS

All trading methods have losing spells. For example, I had a period last year that started off with a string of six straight losing trades, then a mix of losers and winners. Altogether, it took 24 trades before I got back into profit. For me, that equated to about 28 trading days (there were four days when I didn't trade), just over a month.

In years gone by, I used an excellent counter-cyclical trading system on the S&P 500 E-mini futures. Over many years it has been consistently successful. The average length of a trade is about 9 trading days.

A drawdown period of 24 trades with this method (quite likely) means I'm out of pocket for nearly a year – and this is a *good* method!

That's fine if you have another job, and trading is just a hobby. But I trade for a living. I've got food to buy, bills to pay, children to clothe. I know futures trading will never yield a smooth salary income – performance is always lumpy. Even so, I don't want to go for a year without pay.

Since I started day trading, I work through drawdown periods faster and start generating profits again. These days, I don't have too many losing weeks, and negative months are very rare. It's the nearest thing to a steady income I've ever come across in trading.

LESS STRESS

What do you think the combination of instant gratification, reduced risk, and steady profit equates to? You got it; less stress.

WHAT CRISIS?

I'm myopic.

I log on. I watch that first candle being painted on the screen. I wait for a familiar pattern to develop, and if it does I dive into the market, hoping for a quick profit before jumping out again to safety.

I don't care if the market is rising crazily in a resources boom, or collapsing afterwards. I don't care if the sky is falling and subprime lending has sparked Armageddon. It makes no difference to me.

> **All I care about is what is happening to the price of beans, corn or wheat *right now*. This minute.**

Of course, I'm interested if the Dow is off 5%, or wheat hits a historic high. Fascinated. But it makes no difference to what I do or how I do it. I like that.

ARE THERE ANY DRAWBACKS?

Of course there are! Mind you, one old chestnut some commentators come up with is hogwash. The market, they claim, is just too unpredictable in the short term to make a profit. The day trader is doomed to be battered by short-term market noise and sink without a trace. The only hope is to trade longer term.

This is patent nonsense.

Short-term price charts are indistinguishable from long-term charts. Take the scales off, and I challenge those commentators to pick out the difference between a two-minute chart from a single trading session, and a monthly chart covering a period of years. They both exhibit trends, support and resistance levels, ranges and so on.

The real problem with day trading is costs. Any one trade has fixed costs, made up of the broker's commission plus slippage. Long-term traders are looking for big moves and the fixed costs represent only a small percentage of the profit they hope to make. Day traders, on the other hand, are targeting smaller moves with correspondingly smaller profits per contract traded. The fixed cost can easily become a very large percentage of this planned profit, or even consume it entirely.

That's why not all markets are suitable for day trading. You must have good volatility to ensure the target profits are significantly larger than the costs, and good volumes to keep slippage to a minimum. And, as in any business venture, you need to focus on minimising your costs.

CHAPTER 4:
It's All a Gamble

Life's risky

YOU MAY READ books in which authors claim trading is not gambling. It is as though gambling is a dirty word, and they go out of their way to show that trading with discipline using **their** method is something else.

Well, I beg to differ.

Just about everything you do with your money is a gamble.

- You can stick it under your mattress, gambling that a thief won't steal it and its value won't be eroded by inflation.

- You can invest it in a savings account at the bank, gambling they won't run into financial problems and freeze your funds, or just plain lose your money.

- You can buy a diamond, gambling you won't lose it and its market value will not decrease if, for example, somebody floods the market with cheap diamonds.

- You can buy shares, gambling the company whose stock you bought is successful and its share price increases. But then the stock might be called Enron…

- You can buy property, gambling that the value of the property will increase. The large numbers of people around the world with negative equity in their properties are testament to the fact that this bet doesn't always win.

- You can give your money to a hedge fund, gambling that those clever young fellows with their new super-computer-powered-chaos-investment-model won't lose it.

- Or you can open a futures position, gambling that you have picked the market right.

- In fact, when you think about it, much of what you do in life is a gamble. Driving, flying, swimming…

Why is it, then, that some of these things are not considered to be gambling, while others are?

It's all about probabilities. When the probability of something bad happening is very low, most of us tend to discount it and treat it as a certainty. On the other hand, when the risk is big enough to be apparent to all, most people tend to avoid it at all costs, and brand the risk-takers as gamblers.

In finance, the returns from low risk bets are always smaller than the returns from riskier propositions. No one is going to gain stellar returns on an investment with minimal risk. It is akin to a law of nature that high returns require you to take a bigger risk.

My business

I regard my trading as a form of gambling.

Each trading session I place a bet (or, occasionally, I choose to abstain).

There's a chance my bet will be wrong and I will lose money, but if I am right the returns are excellent.

That is the business I have chosen to be in. I succeed if I can put the odds on my side and carefully manage risk.

When it pays to gamble

It pays to gamble when the odds are in your favour. Simple.

The casino owner is glad to gamble with you because the games are all set up to give an edge to the bank. Over time, the casino wins more than it loses.

That doesn't mean the casino never loses. And no trader should ever believe they will win all the time. Managing losses is a vital part of the business, but the successful trader understands that sustaining losses is just part of the winning process.

Putting the odds in your favour

A trading strategy will win in the long run if it has what statisticians call a "positive expectancy". It turns out you can gain positive expectancy in lots of different ways, but here are the guidelines I have chosen:

• I aim to win on at least half my trades, and

• I ensure the average win is bigger than the average loss.

If I meet these two conditions over a long period of time, *and* I manage risk properly (which I'll talk about later), *and* I'm well capitalised, I'm on the road to success.

A winning strategy is only useful if there are plenty of opportunities to use it, so for a profitable business I require a third guideline:

• I aim to find a trade in at least 80% of available trading sessions.

As you will see in a later chapter, I monitor my results against these criteria at the end of each trading month.

CHAPTER 5:
It's All About Managing Risk

AS SOON AS I enter a futures trade, my money is on the line. Futures are leveraged investments, so I can lose a lot more money than I'm putting on the table, *very quickly*, if I don't take the proper precautions.

> You may have noticed that I have a healthy respect for the perils of leveraged investing. If you go into the market without that respect, sooner or later it will hand you a lesson. Don't learn the hard way!

The right physical set-up

There are certain aspects of risk management that are more a question of plain common sense. For example, I owe it to myself to make sure my physical trading set-up is as reliable as it can be, and that I have contingency plans in place to cover myself if the unexpected should occur. This means having an answer to questions like: what will I do if my internet connection fails? (I discuss some aspects of the physical set-up in chapter 18.)

Never trade without a stop loss order in place

Another aspect of risk management is more to do with sensible trading technique. I *never* have an open position without having a stop loss order in place. A stop loss is not a perfect mechanism, but in my opinion it is still the best available protection against the unexpected. Trading without a stop loss is like driving without a seat belt.

The well-disciplined trader knows exactly where the stop is going before entering a trade.

So why not put it in place immediately!

I'm not a fan of mental stops. For one thing, a hopeful trader may fail to take the stop at the right time, or be slow to react in a fast-moving market, or (and this is scary) simply lose the internet connection at the critical moment.

Stops are another reason I prefer day trading. Even in fast market conditions, my stops usually get filled close to the specified level. By contrast, a longer-term trader's stops can easily be filled a long way from the desired level if the market gaps at the open.

How big a bet?

In every trade, the fundamental risk management decision is how big a bet to place.

The bigger the bet I place, the more money I can make. *Or lose...*

If I risk all my capital on each bet, I will go broke when I get my inevitable first loser.

What, then, should I do?

Should I restrict each bet to just 50%, or 25%, or 10% of my capital?

Some kamikaze traders advocate percentage risk, based on a gut feeling that, say, "10% should be OK", or rely on a mathematical calculation called *optimal f*.

> **But never forget: even if a strategy wins half the time – in the long run – it will still have clusters of losses. Sooner or later there will be a run of five or six straight losses.**

How would you feel if you started your trading career with five successive losers when you are risking 10% of your capital per trade?

I'll tell you. You would feel rotten, and you would either give up, or start trading a different system because "this one doesn't work". (And don't forget: Murphy's Law dictates that the moment you stop trading it, the system enters a winning streak.)

My rule of thumb is this:

> *Never risk more than 5% of capital on any one trade. Ideally, risk less than 1.5% of capital on each trade.*

A good strategy with a positive expectancy should keep a trader safe from bankruptcy at the 1.5% level. The 5% level usually gives a good chance of survival, but is still a lot riskier than it sounds.

Why, then, don't I just advocate using 1.5%, and have done with it?

The answer concerns the amount of capital I have for trading.

How much capital?

Say my trading strategy typically requires me to risk about $200 per contract before I take a stop loss. With $10k capital, 1.5% is $150. Thus, I find myself unable to take a typical trade in this market without violating a 1.5% risk level.

With $20k capital, 1.5% is $300, which means I can take the trade with one contract. Two contracts (risking $400) would violate my risk level.

On the other hand, if I decided to use a 5% risk level, I can trade two contracts with a $10k account, because 5% of my capital is $500. Two contracts, risking $400, is within my risk tolerance, but three contracts would increase the risk to $600 – too big.

In practice, many traders do not have enough capital to confine their risk per trade to just 1.5% of capital. My advice is that if you do need to start out risking more than 1.5% because of limited capital, aim to reduce the percentage risked as you accumulate profits.

Don't let margin determine bet size

The margin is a risk management mechanism for my broker, not me. If I am trading corn with a margin (as I write) a little over $2k, my broker will allow me to enter four contracts with a $10k account. That is twice as many contracts as I would trade using the method described above, even at the 5% risk level.

> **Buying as many contracts as possible – given the margin level – will almost inevitably incur far too much risk. Don't do it!**

Conserve trading capital by only placing bets within the specified risk tolerance.

CHAPTER 6:
What Do I Trade?

The business need for futures contracts

TRADE GRAINS FUTURES contracts – soybeans, wheat and corn. There are other grain futures, but they don't trade with enough volume to interest me.

Like all commodities, grains have a cash price at which they can be bought and sold on the open market. The trouble is it is volatile. Storms, droughts, government decisions, wars – all can, and do, cause large price fluctuations.

Farmers who grow grains, and commercial enterprises that use grains as raw materials, realised long ago that they needed a better pricing mechanism to manage their businesses. Just relying on the current cash price left them too exposed to unexpected price movements. They needed to know, *in advance*, what price their grain would be traded for, so they could run their businesses better.

The futures contract was developed as a tool for these entities to manage risk and reduce uncertainty in their business activities.

Long and short

Grain futures contracts are physically settled at the contract expiry date. For example, a corn futures contract is an agreement to exchange 5000 bushels of a standard grade of corn at a specified location when the contract expires, at an agreed price.

A participant is either *long* or *short* the contract. The *long* participant is buying the corn. The *short* participant is the seller.

With grain contracts, food manufacturers typically go *long* to secure their future supply of raw materials at the right time for a known cost. Farmers go *short* to guarantee sales of future harvests at known prices.

Speculators

- The price at which a grain **futures contract** changes hands represents the best guess of the market participants as to what the cash price will be at some future time when the contract expires.

- The **cash price** is the price at which the underlying commodity is trading on the street *now*.

Usually, but not always, the futures price tends to change in a similar fashion to the underlying cash price.

The commercial interests are not the only kids on the block. Indeed, if they were, the futures market would suffer from a lack of liquidity. Liquidity in the market is provided by speculators – such as myself.

I have no interest in either delivering or receiving large quantities of grain, but seek to profit from fluctuations in the price of futures contracts as markets react to changes in the supply and demand balance.

The futures contracts are not personalised, which means they can be readily bought and sold on the futures market. When I buy or sell a contract, I am taking on the associated purchase or delivery obligations. But I can close my position, releasing the obligation, by simply taking the opposite side (selling or buying) in another contract.

The contract

The grains futures markets are amongst the oldest futures markets. The contracts are traded at the Chicago Board of Trade (CBOT), which recently merged with the Chicago Mercantile Exchange (CME) to form the CME Group.

The full contract specifications can be found on the CME Group's web site at **www.cmegroup.com**. A trader must be familiar with the following information:

Table 6.1: Contract specifications for grains

Contract term	Comment
Size and nature of the contract	For example, the soybean futures contract is for 5000 bushels of Number 2 Yellow beans. Wheat and corn contracts are also for 5000 bushels.
Tick size and its value	A tick is the minimum movement permitted in the contract price. For soybeans, wheat and corn it is 0.25 cents per bushel, which equates to $12.50 per contract (5000 × 0.25 cents).
The way in which the price is quoted	Soybean, wheat and corn prices are quoted in cents per bushel (for example, 631.25).
Months when the contract matures	Soybeans have contracts for January, March, May, July, August, September and November each year. Wheat and corn have contracts for March, May, July, September and December.
Last trading day of the contract	For grains this is the fifteenth calendar day of the contract month.

Ticker code(s) for the contract	Often there are two contracts mentioned. One is the traditional floor-traded version, the other is the electronic version. Each has a different code, but I only use the electronic contracts, ZS (soybeans), ZW (wheat) and ZC (corn).
Hours during which the contract is traded	Electronic contracts have extended hours compared to floor-traded contracts, but I only trade during the traditional primary floor trading hours because volumes are too low during extended sessions. The primary trading session for the contracts I trade is 08:30–13:20 US Central Time, Monday to Friday.
Limit information	Grain markets are locked after a limit move. Current limits are $0.70 for soybeans, $0.60 for wheat and $0.30 for corn. However, normal limits may change, or "expand" during exceptional market conditions. (See chapter 13 for a further discussion of how limits work and why it is important to know where they are.)
Contract margin	This specifies the amount of money that must be deposited with the exchange to open, and maintain, positions. It is better to get this figure from your broker because brokerage companies sometimes specify different margin levels from those quoted at the exchange. Margins can, and do, change frequently.

Trade the front contract

Beginner traders are sometimes concerned about getting stuck with a load of grain, but if I always trade the front month (highest trading volume) contract, and ensure I am out of all positions at the end of each trading day, there is no risk of becoming involved in physical delivery issues.

My general rule is never to trade any contract during its expiry month. During the last few days of the month prior to expiry I switch to the new front month. For example, in May 2009 I will be trading the July 2009 corn contract. Towards the end of June I'll switch to the September 2009 contract (the next one available).

> **Note:** the August and September soybeans contracts are lightly traded, so at the end of June it is best to switch directly to the November contract, skipping August and September completely.

Contract codes

My broker (Interactive Brokers) only requires me to know the ticker code of a contract I am trading. Having specified the code, I am presented with menus from which I choose the month and year of expiry.

Some brokers still require the contract to be fully specified by combining the ticker code, a month code, and the year.

Month codes are as follows:

F January

G February

H March

J April

K May

M June

N July

Q August

U September

V October

X November

Z December

For example, I can specify the electronic soybeans contract expiring in November, 2009, as ZSX9 (ZS: electronic soybeans contract; X: November; 9: 2009.)

Not all brokers are consistent in how they do this. Other permutations they may use include ZSX09, ZS9X, and ZS09X.

A word on price

A trader sees three prices mentioned in relation to a futures contract.

- The *bid* is the price at which somebody is prepared to buy a contract.

- The *offer* (or *ask*) is the price at which somebody is prepared to sell.

- The *last trade* is the price at which the last traded contract changed hands.

For example, at any specific moment I might see a last trade of 607.25, with the bid at 607 and the offer at 607.5.

Suppose the last trade is 607.25, the bid is 601 and the offer is 612. This is an example of a wide bid/offer spread. In this situation a trader tries to improve prices by careful order placement. A buyer, rather than just hitting the 612 offer, might put in a bid at, say, 605. Similarly, a seller might put in an offer at 608, hoping that a keen buyer will snap it up.

However, for electronic grain contracts during primary trading sessions, the bid, offer and last trade prices change several times per second! This is especially so at key support and resistance levels (discussed later in this book), when the numbers are simply a blur on the trading screen.

When I refer to *price* in this book, I am referring to the *last trade price*.

Typically, the spread is just 0.25 to 0.5 cents for front month electronic grain contracts during primary trading sessions. Wider spreads are found in lower volume trading situations. For example, when the contract is not the front month contract, or is being lightly traded during an extended trading session.

CHAPTER 7:
What a Speculative Trader Does

GAMBLE ON WHETHER a grain's futures contract price will rise or fall during a single trading session. If I think the price will rise, I open a *long* position. If I think the price will fall, I open a *short* position. Sometimes I'm not sure what to think, and then I sit on the side-lines.

In the futures market I can open long or short positions with equal ease.

- To open a **long trade**, I buy one or more contracts. The position is closed when I sell the same number of contracts.

- To open a **short trade**, I sell one or more contracts. The position is closed when I buy the same number of contracts.

What a short trade means

When I first started trading I had trouble getting my head around the short trade concept.

How could I sell something I don't own?

The thing to remember is that when I go short (sell) a contract, I am taking on the obligation to deliver 5000 bushels of the grain *at the contract delivery date*. If I don't happen to have the grain now, that's no problem. All I must do is buy it *before* the delivery date. And if I can buy it cheaper, then I'll profit on the deal.

The futures market

Grain futures contracts are traded on the Chicago Board of Trade (CBOT). The market simplifies the entire trading process.

First, it provides an electronic marketplace where contracts can be bought and sold very easily.

It automatically nets out my position. If I have bought three contracts and sold four contracts, it knows my net position is short one contract.

Even better, it only requires physical delivery of grain from traders who hold long and short positions at contract expiry. All my transactions are settled by cash.

It works as follows.

A long trade

Suppose I think the price of corn is *rising*, so I buy 4 contracts at 607.25.

Assume I am right, and several minutes later the price moves up to my target and I sell 4 contracts for 611.75.

Since I bought and sold 4 contracts, I no longer have an open position. My money is no longer at risk.

My profit on the trade is 611.75 - 607.25 = 4.5 cents per bushel. There are 5000 bushels per contract, so this equates to $225 per contract. I traded 4 contracts, so the total profit is 4 × $225 = $900. This profit (less brokerage fees) shows up in my trading account the moment the position is closed.

If I was wrong about the price rising, I close the position when the price moves down to a point I have decided will be my stop loss level. Suppose I sell 4 contracts at 605.25.

My loss on the trade is 605.25 - 607.25 = -2.0 cents per bushel, a $100 loss per contract, equating to a $400 loss for the total trade of 4 contracts (before brokerage fees).

A short trade

Suppose I think the price of corn is *falling*, so I *sell* 4 contracts at 607.25.

Assume I am right, and several minutes later the price moves *down* to my target and I *buy* 4 contracts for 602.75.

Since I sold and bought 4 contracts, I no longer have an open position. My money is no longer at risk.

My profit on the trade is 607.25 - 602.75 = 4.5 cents per bushel. There are 5000 bushels per contract, so this equates to $225 per contract. I traded 4 contracts, so the total profit is 4 × $225 = $900. This profit (less brokerage fees) shows up in my trading account the moment the position is closed.

If I was wrong about the price *falling*, I would close the position if the price moved *up* to a price I have decided will be my stop loss level. Suppose I *buy* 4 contracts at 609.25.

My loss on the trade is 607.25 - 609.25 = -2.0 cents per bushel, a $100 loss per contract, equating to a $400 loss for the total trade of 4 contracts (before brokerage fees).

Up or down? It doesn't matter...

You can see that the speculator can bet on rising or falling prices with equal ease.

A long trade makes money if the price goes up, and loses if the price drops. A short trade makes money if the price falls, and loses if the price goes up.

Very simple, and very symmetrical.

I find newcomers to trading usually understand long trading, having bought a few shares somewhere along the line, but must do a bit of work to come to grips with short trading.

Accessing the market

Small speculators like me do not have direct access to the futures exchange; we must go through a futures broker. The broker provides the software interface between me and the marketplace. The software allows me to plan trades, enter orders and manage my account, all via the internet.

A broker charges a commission on each futures trade. My broker charges $3.05 for each transaction. In the first long trade described above, I bought 4 contracts and then sold 4 contracts to close the position. That is 8 transactions in all, so my brokerage fee is 8 × $3.05 = $24.40 for the full trade.

> I use Interactive Brokers (www.interactivebrokers.com) and, as far as I am concerned, they set the benchmark for service, quality and price. (Note that I don't have to be resident in the USA to use a US broker.)

CHAPTER 8:
Charts

Tracking the money

P RICE CHARTS ARE important because they enable me to track the money. Large institutions typically have analysts studying the world grain markets. I don't have the resources and information sources to compete with them. But no matter.

If analysts believe price will rise, the organisations they work for need to act. Their activity is inevitably reflected by changes in price recorded on a price chart.

I visualise myself as a skilled tracker, not a market analyst. My task is to pick up the trail of big money on the chart and follow it to the pot of gold.

Big players do their best to obscure the trail and throw me off their tracks, and frequently succeed. But often enough I manage to hang onto their coat-tails and get my share of the plunder.

Candlestick charts

Charts map the price movement of the grain futures contracts I'm interested in. Although they can be in any time frame, I use two-minute candlestick charts. That means there is a separate candle on the chart representing each two-minute segment of the trading session.

Chart 8.1

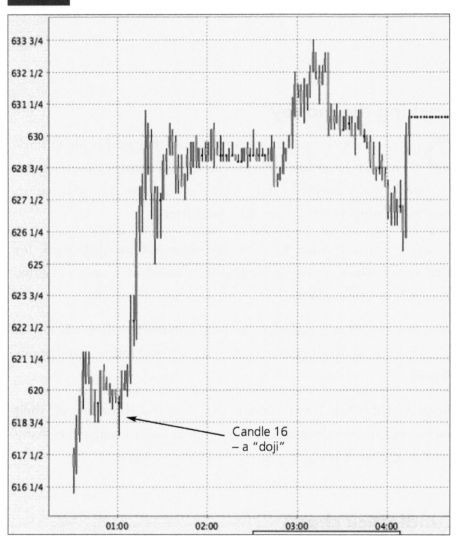

Chart 8.1 is a two-minute candlestick chart showing price movement during a corn session.

The left axis shows price in cents. The horizontal axis shows (Queensland) time. (Sessions run from 09:30 to 13:15 in Chicago, which, depending on summer time, is either 00:30–04:15 or 01:30–05:15 here in Queensland.)[2]

Each vertical candle on this chart represents price movement during a two-minute period.

Candlestick charts typically have a body between the opening and closing prices of the period (in this case two minutes), with a tail up to the highest price and a tail down to the lowest point of the period.

By convention the body is a thick line and the tails are thin lines. The colour of the body indicates the direction of overall price movement during the period.

You can use any colour scheme that appeals to you. I use a blue body to show a rising price, a red body for a falling price, and black tails.

Interpreting a candlestick chart

Look at the first vertical line. I'll call it candle 1.

- **Candle 1** tells me the price story during the first two minutes of the trading session. The body is red, so I know the closing price was lower than the opening price. Looking at the red body, I see price opened at 617.5 and closed at 617. From the tails, I can see that price reached a high of 617.75 and a low of 616 during this period.

- **Candle 2** tells the price story during the next two minutes. It is blue, so I know the closing price was higher than the opening price

---

2   Since 2013, Chicago sessions run from 0830–1320.

for the two-minute period. The body shows price opened at 617 and closed at 618.5. The tails tell me the lowest point was 616.75 and the high point was 619.

- **Candle 3** tells me what happened during the next two minutes. The blue body shows me price opened at 618.25 and closed at 619.75. The bottom tail tells me the low point was 618. The lack of a top tail indicates that the price closed at the high point for the period, 619.75.

Sometimes there is no body. Look at candle 16. The body is a single dot on the bar. This indicates that the opening and closing prices were the same: 619.5. The tails show me the high for the period was 619.75 and the low was 618.25. This type of candle is called a *doji*.

> **Interactive Brokers' trading platform provides me with great charting facilities allowing me to display this kind of chart as it forms in real-time. I use it to look for specific patterns developing, which indicate to me when to trade, which direction to trade in, where my stop loss should be and where to set my target. How I do this is explained in the following chapters.**

CHAPTER 9:
Support and Resistance

I LIKE TO TRADE the open. That's when the greatest volumes hit the market and price often seems to swing wildly. To me it is a time of opportunity!

But it is also a time when I don't have a lot of information to go on. Maybe the market has opened higher or lower than yesterday's close, but I don't find that gives me much of a clue as to where it will go during the session.

The challenge is to find my bearings and identify potential trades as quickly as possible. This chapter gives a brief overview of the principles I rely on to do this. The next chapter gives the precise rules.

Turning points on charts are significant

Charts reveal levels at which the market has previously turned. These levels may be price peaks the market reached before pulling back, or low points reached before the market bounced. The peaks form resistance and low points form support.

> **Support and resistance levels are the places where most traders choose to fight their battles.**

Whenever price approaches an obvious support and resistance level, a battle ensues between the bulls and the bears. Bulls are buying, bears are selling. The battle is witnessed by the day trader who sees a flurry of transactions whenever a support or resistance level is approached.

Figure 9.1

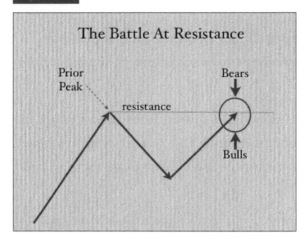

Figure 9.2

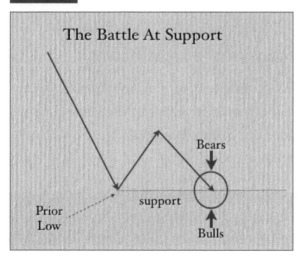

Who wins the battle?

The circled areas in figures 9.1 and 9.2 show the battle zones at the support and resistance levels. Within these zones the battle sways to and fro, with market participants employing different kinds of tactics to try and get the best entries.

When one side gives way, there is often a price spike as the other side surges through the breached defences. Figure 9.3 shows a battle at resistance won by the bulls, and figure 9.4 shows the same battle won by bears.

Figure 9.3

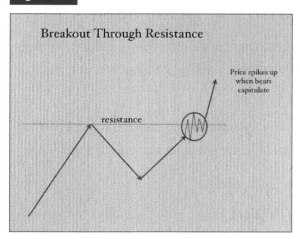

Figure 9.4

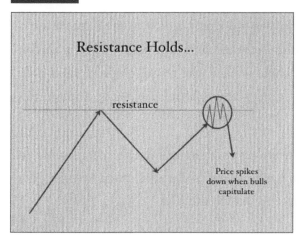

There is no way of knowing which side will win these battles. But the oldest saying in trading is "the trend is your friend", and this gives a clue about which side to back.

The basic idea is that trends have momentum and are quite hard to stop. So, in an up-trending market, bulls have the edge. In a down-trending market, bears have the edge. (Only an edge – not a guarantee!)

How this relates to trading at the open

When the grains futures open, there is almost always a flurry of early activity. The high point of this early activity is resistance, and the low point is support.

In fact, although intermediate support and resistance levels are formed during a session, the only ones I ever concern myself with are:

- **resistance** at the session high point
- **support** at the session low point.

Having established support and resistance levels, I need to get a feel for the trend. Is it up or down?

Remember, I am looking at two-minute candles as they appear on a chart. When the first candle is complete, I can get my first tentative read on the trend. If the candle is blue, the trend is up. If the candle is red, the trend is down. (Check my colour convention for candles in chapter 8.)

After a few candles have been completed, trends are often easier to pick. The classic uptrend has a series of candles, each with higher highs and higher lows than the last (figure 9.5).

Figure 9.5

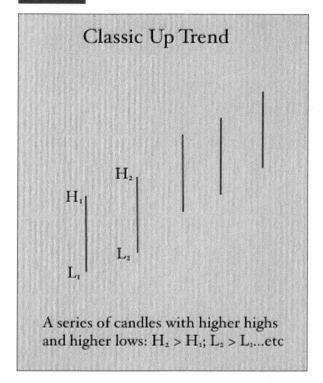

Classic Up Trend

H_1

L_1

H_2

L_2

A series of candles with higher highs and higher lows: $H_2 > H_1$; $L_2 > L_1$...etc

The classic downtrend has a series of candles, each with lower lows and lower highs than the last (figure 9.6).

Figure 9.6

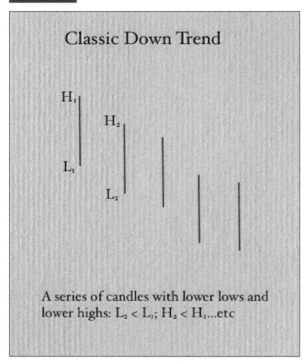

Classic Down Trend

H₁
H₂
L₁
L₂

A series of candles with lower lows and lower highs: $L_2 < L_1$; $H_2 < H_1$...etc

Real-life charts seldom look like carefully drawn diagrams, but nevertheless it is my job to form a view about trend direction right from the outset of the session.

The trading idea

Once I have established support and resistance levels (at the session's low and high points), and I have taken a view on the trend direction, my plan is to trade the first significant breakout (in either direction).

If it is a breakout above resistance I go long. If it is a breakout below support, I go short.

Support and resistance is the key, trading with the trend is the intention. Now, read on for the specific rules.

CHAPTER 10:
Entry Rules

Bias

DURING THE TRADING session, I have a bias of either up, down or neutral. Initially, I am neutral, but I aim to adopt a bias when the first bar is completed:

- If the body of the candlestick is **blue**, which on my charts represents upward movement during the two-minute time period, my bias is *up* (long).

- If the body of the candlestick is **red**, my bias is *down* (short).

- If the candlestick is a **doji**, I stay *neutral* and let the second bar dictate my initial bias.

Pullbacks

I enter breakout trades in the direction of a trend after a pullback has occurred.

A pullback is just that: a retracement from a previous high in an uptrend (when my bias is up), or from a previous low in a downtrend (when my bias is down).

After the market makes a new session high at point A, I define a pullback as occurring if at least two consecutive following candles have lower highs than point A.

Figure 10.1

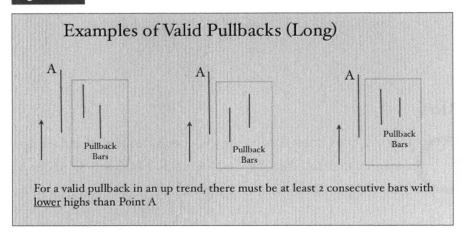

Examples of Valid Pullbacks (Long)

For a valid pullback in an up trend, there must be at least 2 consecutive bars with lower highs than Point A

Similarly, if the market makes a new session low at point B, then I define a pullback as occurring if at least two of the following candles have higher lows than point B.

Figure 10.2

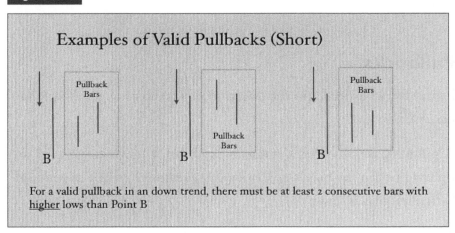

Examples of Valid Pullbacks (Short)

For a valid pullback in an down trend, there must be at least 2 consecutive bars with higher lows than Point B

If, after making a new high at point A, the pullback is so extreme that point B is penetrated, creating a new session low, then I change my bias from up to down, and await a valid pullback from the new lows.

Figure 10.3

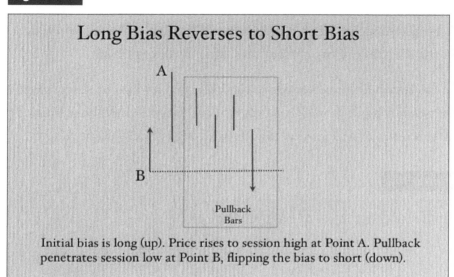

Long Bias Reverses to Short Bias

A

B

Pullback
Bars

Initial bias is long (up). Price rises to session high at Point A. Pullback
penetrates session low at Point B, flipping the bias to short (down).

Similarly, if the pullback from session point B is so extreme that point
A is penetrated, I switch bias from down to up and await a pullback
from the new highs.

Figure 10.4

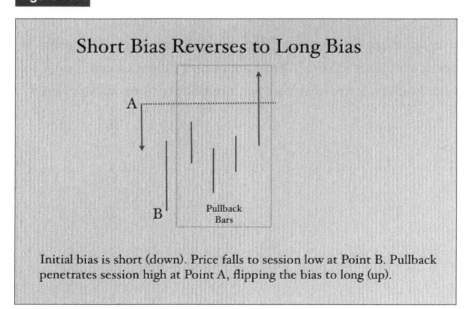

Short Bias Reverses to Long Bias

A

B

Pullback
Bars

Initial bias is short (down). Price falls to session low at Point B. Pullback
penetrates session high at Point A, flipping the bias to long (up).

Breakouts

A breakout occurs when a previous session high or low is penetrated, in the direction of my current bias, after a valid pullback.

In an uptrending market where my bias is up and point A represents the session high, a breakout occurs if the market rises above point A after a series of at least two candles with highs below point A.

Figure 10.5

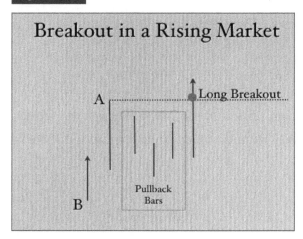

In a downtrending market where my bias is down and point B represents the session low, a breakout occurs if the market drops below point B after a series of at least two candles with lows above point B.

Figure 10.6

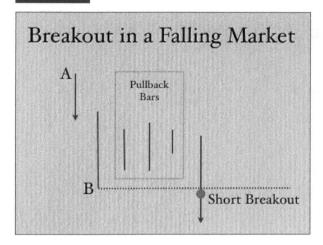

Trade trigger

I await the first breakout in the session and enter a trade in the direction of the breakout. If no breakout occurs, I don't trade.

EXCEPTION: SECOND CANDLE PULLBACK FOLLOWED BY THIRD CANDLE BREAKOUT

I do make one exception to the general definition above, and this is because the early action in the trading session (the first four or five minutes) is very busy and fast moving. If the first candle moves in a particular direction, the second candle is a pullback, and then the third candle resumes the move in the original direction, then I treat the single second candle pullback as valid, and the third candle therefore provides a valid breakout.

Figure 10.7

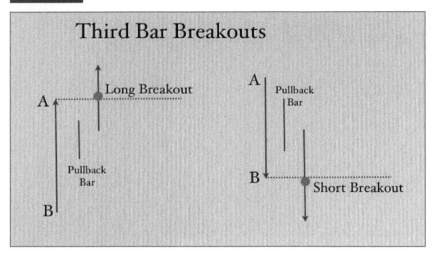

Note that in this scenario the second candle is always an inside candle (where its high and low are both within the extremes set by the preceding bar).

This exception came about because I used to use one-minute candles for the first six minutes of trading, to better accommodate the initial flurry of activity. I used my standard rules with the one-minute bar, but it was a hassle switching between one-minute and two-minute charts. When I noticed that allowing these third candle breakouts on the two-minute charts gave roughly the same results, I adopted this technique.

SOME EXAMPLES

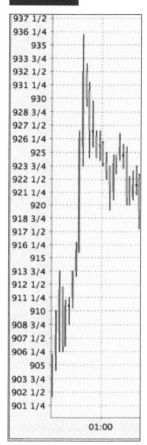

Chart 10.1

Candle 1 is blue, giving me a long bias. The first three candles push higher, then candles 4–7 pull back from the initial high (913.75). A pullback is what I am waiting for, and now I anticipate a resumption of the move. When price pushes back up to 914 (a tick over the initial high) in candle 8, I go long.

Chart 10.2

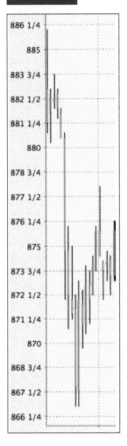

In Chart 10.2, candle 1 is red, indicating a bias to the short side. Price falls to 880.25 in candle 2, then pulls back (up) in bars 3–5. The pullback puts me on the alert for a resumption of the downward move. When price hits 880, one tick below the initial low, in candle 6, I go short.

Chart 10.3

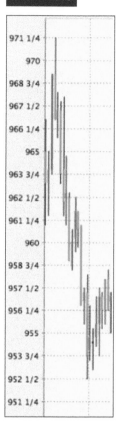

In chart 10.3, bar 1 is down (red), indicating a short bias. Candle 2 pulls back with a higher low, so I immediately look for a straightforward short trade. However, candle 3 breaks up through the top of the first candle which changes the bias to long, and I await further developments. Candle 4 continues up, but candles 5–8 represent a pullback from the new high. However, when candle 9 penetrates back down through the session low I change my bias back to short. Candle 10 makes a new low, then candles 12 and 13 make a valid pullback. Candle 14 breaks out to the downside and when price hits 958.25, one tick below the low in candle 10, I go short.

Chart 10.4

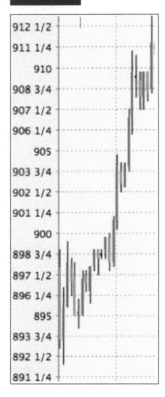

In chart 10.4, the first candle is down (red) establishing a downward bias. Candle 2 continues the move down, but candle 3 reverses and breaks the first candle upwards, changing the bias to up. Candles 4–12 constitute a valid pullback from the new high, before candle 13 breaks upwards, and I go long at 899.75.

Chart 10.5

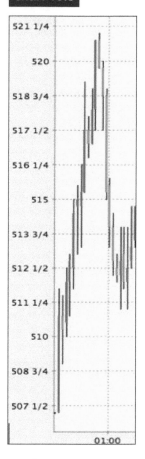

In chart 10.5, candle 1 is blue, rising to 511.75, establishing a long bias. Candle 2 is a pullback (with a lower high). A second candle pullback needs no further confirmation, so I am on the alert to a possible long trade if candle 3 breaks upwards. Sure enough, candle 3 does move up and I go long when price reaches 512, one tick over the high of candle 1.

Chart 10.6

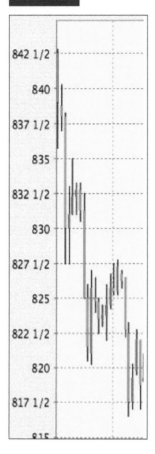

In chart 10.6, candle 1 is red, falling to 836, establishing a short bias. Candle 2 has a higher low, qualifying as a pullback. Again, this is a second candle pullback, signalling a possible short trade if candle 3 breaks downwards. In this case it does, and I go short when price hits 835.75, one tick under the low of candle 1.

CHAPTER 11:
Managing the Trade

L ONG-TERM TRADERS, WHEN asked by a rookie for their secret of trading success, might close their eyes and rock gently back and forward, before dispensing a pearl of wisdom along the lines of:

Let winners run and cut losses quickly.

The rookie nods politely, as one does in the presence of eccentric greatness, before racing off with a puzzled frown to pursue his or her strenuous pursuit of the infallible entry.

So, what is this nugget of conventional trading wisdom all about?

It refers to the twin temptations of protecting profitable trades by closing them before they have time to blossom and allowing losing trades to linger in the hope that they will turn round and become winners. Yielding to these temptations results in your average win being smaller than your average loss. In most cases, this is a recipe for disaster.

You might like to glance back at chapter 4. Remember the first two principles for putting the odds in my favour:

1. Win at least half the time.

2. Ensure my average win is bigger than my average loss.

In chapter 9, I showed you how I get into trades. But that is only half the battle. It's what you do next that ultimately determines your profitability in this business.

The parameters are under my control

Having entered a trade, its probability of success is determined entirely by how I manage it. If I set a small target with a large stop loss, I'll get a high winning percentage with a poor average win to average loss ratio.

Conversely, an ambitious target in comparison to the stop will give a much lower probability of success, but a high average win to average loss ratio.

An important aside

Before I go through the mechanism I use to decide where to set my stop loss and target levels, I need to mention one of the most important techniques I use to help me stick to my management plan.

> **Whenever I've entered a trade, I immediately enter a stop order at my calculated loss point, and a limit order to take profits at my calculated target level. I then walk away from the trade, and let it work, without changing these levels.**

It is difficult for me to over-emphasise how important this is in my trading success.

- It is how I let winners run and cut losses quickly.

- It is how I ensure that every bet I make is based on an identical situation to every other bet.

- It is how I fight the almost irresistible urge to tinker with each trade.

- It is how I save hours of staring at the screen, willing the market to move in my direction. (And in my case, as I live in Australia and trade in the middle of the night, it allows me to get hours of extra sleep.)

In the long run, I don't believe I gain any benefit from watching trades for hours on end.

Setting the stop and limit levels

OK, I know how to initiate a breakout trade, and I've established that I should immediately set a stop loss and a profit-taking order when I enter the trade.

But what levels should the stop and limit be set at?

Some sessions are volatile with large moves, calling for bigger targets and wider stops. Others are less volatile, requiring smaller targets with tighter stops. The only clue I have as to the type of session I'm in is the action preceding my entry.

Therefore, I set my stop and target levels based on the swings already seen on the chart.

DEFINING R – THE RANGE

Recall that I enter a long trade after a *pullback* from resistance, followed by a move back up through the resistance level, or a short trade after a *pullback* from support followed by a break back down through the support level. To get an idea of where to set my target and stop levels I determine a range (r).

One end of the range is always the breakout (support or resistance) level. To find the other end of the range, I follow this procedure:

> **For a long trade, I look back to find the low of the last candle which had a lower low *and* lower high than its immediately preceding candle.**

Figure 11.1

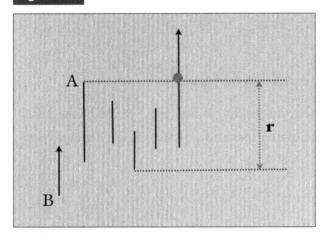

For a short trade, I look back to find the high of the last candle which had a higher low *and* higher high than its immediately preceding candle.

Figure 11.2

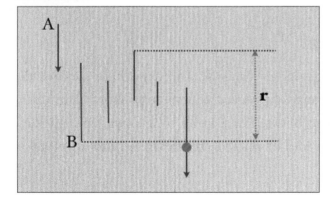

Often enough this will be the extreme point of the most recent pullback (Fig 11.1 and Fig 11.2), but sometimes it is not (Fig 11.3). Occasionally, no candle matching the criteria is found, in which case take r as the full session range (Fig 11.4).

Figure 11.3

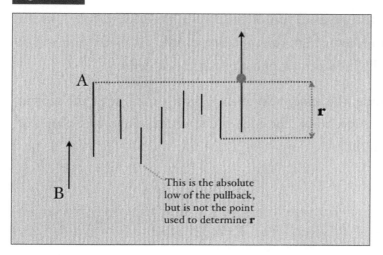

This is the absolute low of the pullback, but is not the point used to determine **r**

Figure 11.4

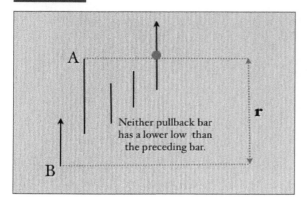

Neither pullback bar has a lower low than the preceding bar.

Second candle pullback followed by third candle breakout

The market action is at its fastest during the first few minutes of trading. For that reason, if the second candle is a pullback, I consider it valid without a second confirming pullback candle.

In this case, the pullback candle is always an inside candle, with a higher low and lower high than the first candle. As usual, one end of the range is the breakout (support or resistance) level.

For a long trade, the lower end of the range is the low of the second candle. For a short trade, the higher end of the range is the high of the second candle.

Figure 11.5

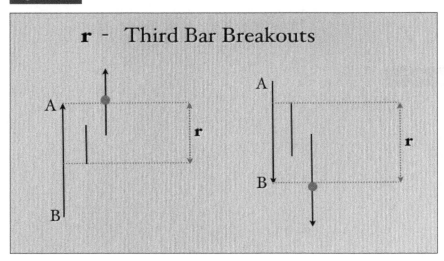

EXAMPLES

Charts 11.1 to 11.6 all have the breakout point and the range r marked on them.

Chart 11.1

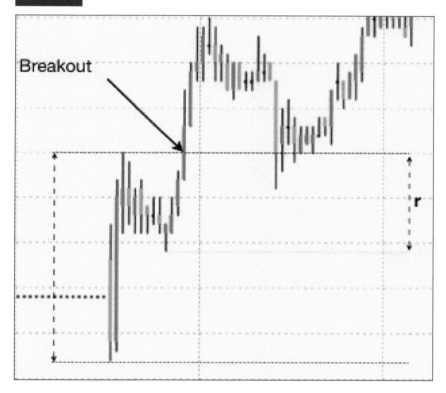

Chart 11.2

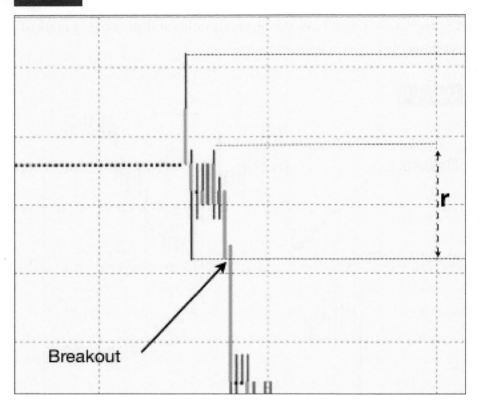

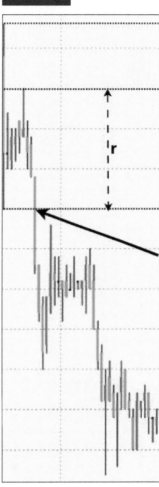

Chart 11.5

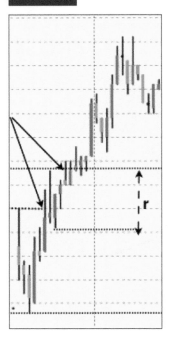

Chart 11.6

Determining the profit and stop loss levels

Once I have determined the range, finding the profit and stop loss levels is simple. I typically set my:

- **stop loss** somewhere between 0.5r and 1r, and the

- **profit level** between 1.5r and 3r.

I usually aim for a profit of two to three times the risk. The trading examples in this book have stops set to 0.5r and profit targets at 1.5r.

Equally valid combinations would be 1r : 2.5r, or 0.7r : 2r. Different markets tend to have different optimal combinations.

Personality comes into it as well. Wider stops with smaller targets (for example, 1r : 2r) win more often, at the expense of a poorer win to loss ratio. Tight stops with big targets (for example, 0.5r : 4r) score big wins, but don't win so often.

A strong argument in favour of specialising in one or two markets, which you get to know intimately, is that you get a feel for how far price tends to run after breakouts, as well as the likely depth of retrenchments.

- Markets that are breaking out of ranges with **high momentum** can be traded with tighter stops.

- **Quieter markets** often break out in a much choppier fashion, and it pays to have wider stops.

Your chosen market may have periods of both kinds of activity, so from time to time it may be necessary to adjust your target level and stop loss parameters, but resist doing this too often.

I prefer trading a market showing strong momentum on breakouts, and I enjoy working with the grain markets for this reason. One or the other of them is normally on the move. If soybeans quieten down, wheat might go for a run. Sometimes, beans and wheat get too hot and then corn is often a great option.

CHAPTER 12:
Implementing the Plan

How do I put the strategies described in the last two chapters into practice?

The answer is that, having logged onto my broker's trading platform, monitored the charts, and planned my trade, I must enter the appropriate orders into the system.

Traders employ several different types of orders to implement various strategies, but I only use three of them:

- **Market Order**

Which executes immediately at the best price available. If the market is open, execution is guaranteed but the price is not.

- **Limit Order**

Which executes at a specific price (or better). A buy limit order specifies the highest price (below current market price) at which I am prepared to buy; a sell limit order specifies the minimum price (above current market) at which I am prepared to sell. With limit orders, the price is guaranteed but execution is not. The market may never reach my limit, and even if it does my order is not necessarily filled (depending on the number of transactions at that price).

- **Stop Order**

Which is used to limit my losses or to enter breakout trades. A buy stop order is placed at a price above the current market. If price rises to the stop price, a market buy order is triggered. A sell stop order is placed at a price below the current market. If price drops to the stop price, a market sell order is triggered. Neither execution nor price is guaranteed with stop orders.

Example: order types

Suppose the corn futures price is 600.

- If the market is open and I enter a market buy order, my order will be filled immediately. However, because prices can change quickly, I may typically be filled anywhere between 599 and 601, or even further away from 600. That's what is meant by saying execution is guaranteed, but price is not.

- If I enter a limit buy order at, say, 599 my order will only be completed if it can be filled for 599 or less. If price does not drop below 599, or my order cannot be filled at 599, the order is not executed. Thus, price is guaranteed (I know I won't pay more than 599), but execution is not.

- If I enter a buy stop order at, say, 602 my order will be triggered if any contracts change hands at 602 or above. When a transaction at 602 (or higher) is detected, the stop order immediately becomes a market buy order. As explained above, the fill price for market orders cannot be guaranteed. So it would not be surprising if a buy stop order at 602 is eventually filled at, say, 602.5. If price never rises to 602, the stop order is not triggered and the order is not filled. The fact that a stop order may never be triggered, and, if it is triggered, the actual price of the transaction is not certain, illustrates what is meant by saying that, with stop orders, neither execution nor price is guaranteed.

Slippage

Slippage is the difference between the price I hope to get in the market and the price I actually get. In my kind of trading, it is a problem encountered with stop orders.

In a perfect world, there would be no slippage. In practice, there is nearly always some, and it is a significant expense for a day trader. Suppose price is currently at 600 and I want to go long if it reaches 602 cents.

I enter a buy stop order at 602. As explained above, especially in fast market conditions, the order may be filled at a higher value, say 602.5.

That represents a $0.50 cent ($25 per contract) slippage. Any profit I make will be $25 less than expected. Any loss incurred will be $25 more than I anticipated. Even a $0.25 cent slippage ($12.50) represents an expense more than double the brokerage I pay on the transaction.

Initiating a trade

All my trades are initiated if a resistance level is penetrated (long) or a support level is penetrated (short).

This is easily achieved by entering a buy stop order one pip above the resistance level for a long trade, or a stop sell order one pip below the support level for a short trade.

If the resistance or support levels are penetrated, the stop orders are triggered. But if price fails to penetrate the levels, the orders are never activated and can be cancelled.

Management of a long trade

Assume a buy stop order was triggered and I am in a long trade. For example, I am long corn at 600. From the charts, I have calculated r and worked out that my stop loss level is 598 and my target is to take a profit at 604.

To implement the stop loss I enter a *sell stop* order at 598. To implement my profit taking order, I enter a *sell limit* order at 604.

Conceivably, neither of these orders will execute during the trading session. Price may stay in the range between 598 and 604. However, whatever happens, I want to exit the trade at the close of the session, because I am a day trader.

This requirement is implemented with a sell market order, using the Good After Time (GAT) facility. This feature allows me to specify the time the order is to be submitted. Since the grain sessions close at 13:15 US Central Time, I might choose to submit the order at 13:10, five minute before the close.[3]

If this were all I did, I would need to sit and watch the trade. Otherwise, unexpected results could occur. For instance, suppose my trade is successful and the sell limit order executes as intended to close my position. The problem is that the stop order is still sitting in the market. If price subsequently falls back and triggers the sell stop loss order, I would find myself in an unwanted short position.

---

3   I used to go much closer to the end of the session, but nowadays orders for the last minute are rejected.

ONE CANCELS ALL (OCA)

This problem is avoided by setting up the three orders in a One Cancels All (OCA) group. Not all brokers provide this facility, but it is a blessing to the day trader. Your trades are set up like this:

OCA Group:

1. Sell Stop 598

2. Sell Limit 604

3. Sell Market GAT 13:15

As soon as any one of these orders executes, the other two are automatically cancelled. It is this great facility that allows me to automate my exit strategy and walk away from the screen once my trade is working!

Management of a short trade

The short trade is just a mirror image of the long trade. For example, I am short corn at 600. From the charts, I have calculated r and worked out that my stop loss level is 602 and my target is to take a profit at 596.

All I need to do is set up the following OCA Group:

OCA Group:

1. Buy Stop 602

2. Buy Limit 596

3. Buy Market GAT 13:15

Easy!

CHAPTER 13:
My Trading Calculator

O NCE A TRADING session starts, the action is fast and furious and I haven't got much time to spare. I don't want to be in a position of writing down ranges, calculating stop and target levels by hand, or manually working out how many contracts I can take.

Figure 13.1

1177.00	
1169.75	

LONG	
Contracts	4
Entry	1177.25
Target	1193.75
Stop	1173.50
Target Profit	3150
Target Risk	900

SHORT	
Contracts	4
Entry	1169.50
Target	1153.00
Stop	1173.25
Target Profit	3150
Target Risk	900

Price	1181.00
Change	-2
Limit	70
Capital	25000
Rate	1.1994
Margin	4725
Upper Limit	1253.00
Prev. Close	1183.00
Lower Limit	1113.00
Stop factor	0.5
Profit factor	1.5
Fixed Risk	3.0%

Figure 13.1 is a screenshot of a spreadsheet calculator I use to do this work for me.

Setup begins about ten minutes before the trading session opens. At this time I ensure all the information in the bottom half of the spreadsheet is up to date and correct, as follows.

PRICE, CHANGE

I access the price quote for the contract I'm trading. This quote shows the current price and the change from the previous day's close. I put each of these numbers into the *Price* and *Change* lines on the spreadsheet.

LIMIT

I visit the Exchange's website (**www.cmegroup.com/trading/Price-Limit-Update.html**) to check the daily limit for the product I am trading. I check this daily because limits can expand and contract automatically during volatile periods. The correct value is entered in the *Limit* line. The spreadsheet then calculates and displays the correct values in the *Upper Limit*, *Previous Close* and *Lower Limit* lines. (See pages 107–110 for more information about limits.)

CAPITAL

I view my account details and put the current value of my trading capital into the *Capital* line. As I nominate Australian dollars as my base currency, this figure is in AUD. In the next line (*Rate*) I put the current exchange rate from Australian to US dollars. (If I were simply trading in USD, the exchange rate would be set to 1.000.)

MARGIN

Now I visit my broker's website (**goo.gl/jrR9Mr**)[4] and ensure that the *Margin* for the product I am trading has not been changed. The correct figure is entered into the *Margin* line.

STOP, PROFIT TARGET

I check the *Stop Factor* and *Profit Factor* lines to ensure these values are what I want them to be. They should already be set correctly because, as explained in chapter 11, they should only be changed rarely. Recall that these factors are used in combination with the range r to calculate the stop level and profit target level.

FIXED RISK

Finally, I check the *Fixed Risk* is what I want it to be. Again, this value is rarely changed. Recall that this is the greatest percentage of my account I am prepared to risk on any one trade (see chapter 5), and is used to calculate the number of contracts to trade.

> **These are like pre-flight checks that pilots do. I check each line carefully; even when I feel sure there will be no change from the last time I saved the spreadsheet at the end of the preceding trading session.**

It only takes a few minutes, but provides the first bit of structure to my day.

---

4   In case of changes to Google's link-shortening service in future, for reference the full URL is: **individuals.interactivebrokers.com/en/trading/marginRequirements/ margin.php?p=f&ib_entity=llc**

OTHER PARAMETERS

To ensure the calculator can be tailored to any market, there are other values that can be set, but I have placed them out of sight because they are not values I check each day.

There is a default value for **slippage** (in pips) to assume when a stop order is triggered. I generally set this to 1, although it is better to set it to 2 when trading wheat.

There is a default minimum acceptable **Reward/Risk ratio**. I normally have this set to 1.75. It means that if my target profit is not at least 1.75 times the target risk, I get a message saying "No Trade" in the Contracts line.

There are also values for **Pip Size**, **$ per pip**, and **$ per point**. These values are set to 0.25, $12.50 and $50 by default, correct for soybeans, wheat and corn futures markets, and as it happens also correct for the popular S&P 500 E-mini futures contract. If you wanted to use this calculator for trading some other market, these values simply must be reset to the correct values.

UPDATING RANGE R

Once the trading session opens, I constantly update the two values in the area with a black background at the top of the spreadsheet. These values are the upper and lower levels of the range, r, discussed in chapter 11, and may need to be altered several times as the chart begins to form.

When the range values are entered, the two central areas of the calculator provide all the information I need to take either the long or short trade. I am provided with the:

- **number** of contracts to order

- **entry point** where the order is to be placed

- **target** where a profit-taking limit order is to be placed

- **stop** where the stop loss order is placed

- **target profit** and the **target risk,** both expressed in dollars.

All these values are calculated according to the principles set out in this book.

AN INVALUABLE TOOL

This one tool allows me to quickly determine all the information required to properly implement my trading plan. (The calculator automatically prevents any orders that would violate the session limits, provided it is set up correctly before the session starts.)

If you are going to trade fast moving markets, you need a tool like this. Believe me, trying to do these calculations with pencil and paper when you are in the middle of an adrenalin-pumping session just does not work, and the consequences of mistakes can be very expensive.

> **If you are good with spreadsheets, it is a simple matter to put together your own version. Otherwise you can download mine for a modest fee (*www.tradingcalculator. com.au*).**

FURTHER COMMENT ON SESSION LIMITS

You may be a little confused by the emphasis I place on knowing the daily limits for the markets I trade. I explained the concept of limits in chapter 6 when I described the contract, but let me go through that in more detail so that you can see why they are so important.

The price of grain futures contracts is only allowed to move a certain amount in any one day. If price moves up or down by this amount the market is locked. It remains locked until price moves back the other way, or until trading opens on the following day.

The current limits for grains are given in the following table.

Table 13.1: Limit moves on grain contracts

Grain	Limit (c)
Corn	30
Wheat	60
Soybeans	70

Thus, if corn closed at 600 yesterday, it will not be permitted to trade higher than 630 or lower than 570 today.

EXPANDING LIMITS

Furthermore, under Exchange rules, the limit expands following a limit move. For example, if corn finishes today's session at 570 (ie, limit down), tomorrow's limits are expanded to 45 cents. The contract is permitted to trade between 615 and 525 tomorrow. Assume the market rebounds tomorrow and ends the day limit up at 615. Limits are expanded a second time to 70 cents. The market is allowed to trade the next day between 685 and 545. Regardless of more limit moves, no further expansion of limits is permitted.

When there is a day without a limit move, the limits are reduced to the preceding level; from 70 down to 45, and from 45 down to 30.

For wheat the limits are 60, 90 and 135. For soybeans they are 70, 105 and 160. As mentioned above, this information is published on the CME Group web site (**www.cmegroup.com/trading/Price-Limit-Update.html**). I *always* check it, because it is subject to change.

The reason for expanded limits is to handle periods of high volatility when the normal limits can cause the market to function inefficiently. Most of the time, markets trade within the standard limits for months on end. Then a period of volatility comes along, and limits may be hit regularly for a period of weeks, even months.

THE IMPORTANCE OF KNOWING THESE LIMITS

The trader needs to know the daily limits to avoid placing orders that cannot be filled. For example, I might go long and, based on my calculation using r, enter a profit-taking limit order to sell at 632, unaware of a 630 limit. It would be impossible for my limit order to execute!

The trading calculator never recommends an order outside the day's limits.

Also, beware of taking positions when the stop is close to a limit. For example, suppose the corn price opens limit up at 630 and then starts to move down. Say I get a signal to go short at 625 and calculate the stop loss should be set at 629.5.

I am placing myself in grave danger if I take this trade!

If the trade goes against me, my stop loss will trigger when a transaction takes place at 629.5, but if the market is moving quickly the buy order to exit the position may be unable to execute before the market locks at 630.

If the market remains locked for the rest of the session, I cannot exit the position and will suffer a sleepless night wondering where the market will open next day (or in the thinly traded after-hours session). I might be able to exit at the open of the next session, but it is quite conceivable that the market will gap up dramatically and open at, say, 645, so that I lose 15 cents ($750 per contract) more than expected.

The nightmare scenario is that the market remains locked limit up for several sessions. That is, it opens the next session limit up at 675 and I never get a chance to exit. Then it opens the following session limit up at 745, and I still can't exit! Admittedly this is an unusual situation, but it does happen, so don't risk it!

> **Know where the limits are, and don't put stops near them.**

If you ever get stuck in this nightmare scenario, you can protect yourself to some extent by buying call options (since the option market doesn't lock), but it will still be an expensive proposition.

The trading calculator prominently displays the upper and lower limits for the day.

CHAPTER 14:
My Trading Screen

FIGURE 14.1 SHOWS how I set up my trading screen. The key features are described below.

Figure 14.1

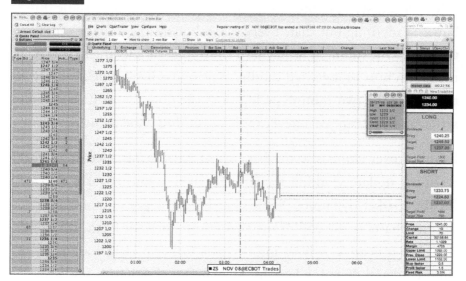

Candlestick charts

The large window in the centre of the screen displays the two-minute candlestick chart for the market I'm trading.

This can be completely customised, so the colour scheme and general layout can be set up to satisfy my personal preferences. Naturally I can customise the chart to show volume, zillions of indicators, Fibonacci retracements and goodness knows what else, but I don't bother with any of that.

All I want is a simple, uncluttered screen showing two-minute candlestick bars. I make it as big as I can, so that the scale is clear. I also have the cross-hair function active so that when I place the cursor on a candle, I can see the high, low, open and close for the candle in a separate little window.

REAL-TIME PAINTING

The most important thing about the charts is that they update in real-time. Of course, a picture of the chart makes it look like a static thing, but it is anything but that. Every second or so, the current candle is updated. One moment it may be a short blue candle, the next it may transform into a longer red candle, as price oscillates quickly. Only at the end of the two-minute period does the final shape of the candle settle, and you can see a new candle beginning to be painted.

I cannot over-emphasise the benefits of having this speedy, smooth real-time update working for you. It enables you to get a real feel for the market dynamics. Some charting packages only update two-minute charts at the end of the two-minute period; I can work with that, but it is not nearly so informative. Other packages are not real-time at all and there is a lengthy delay before the chart is updated.

I couldn't work with that!

In fact, it would be downright dangerous.

> **There are many sources of good charting software. I use the excellent charting facilities that are part of Interactive Brokers' standard trading platform (Trader Work Station – TWS).**

Simple order entry

The window on the left of my screen in Fig 14.1 is the Book Trader window. As you can see, it shows all the price levels, and when the session is open it is updated very rapidly in real-time so that I can always see the current trade price.

I can also see the number of limit orders sitting at the nearest four price levels, but the market moves so quickly I've never found a useful way of using this information.

My main use of this window is to enter orders quickly. A single left click on the Bid column enters a Buy Limit order, a left click on the Ask column enters a Sell Limit order. Right clicks enter Stop instead of Limit orders. Clicking on an existing order cancels it immediately. (A pulldown menu at the top of the window lets me quickly select the default number of contracts used in each order.) Note that this window can look and act differently depending on your choice of customisation settings.

> The Book Trader window shown is specific to the Interactive Brokers' TWS trading platform. If you use a different broker, make sure that there is an analogous function, because single-click order entry and cancellation is a must-have facility for day trading the grain markets.

Trading calculator

The narrow window on the right of my trading screen is the trading calculator, the spreadsheet described fully in chapter 13.

TWS Trading Window

In the top right of my trading screen you can just see a small part of the basic TWS trading window. Having it there is handy, because one click on that area brings the full window to the front at the top of the screen. Clicking back on the chart hides it again.

The only time I use this window is when I am entering an OCA group. I demonstrate this in the case study described in chapter 15.

Another handy feature is the clock displayed in the small part of the TWS trading window that is always visible. This clock is updated in real-time and is therefore more reliable than the system clock on your PC.

CHAPTER 15:
A Case Study

I T'S ALL VERY well writing about this stuff, but what does it look like in practice?

To give you a taste of the real thing, I took a series of screenshots while I was trading. It's not something I like to do, because any distraction is a bad thing, but I hope you find it beneficial. I decided to focus exclusively on soybeans. Normally, I put off this decision until I've observed the open and see which of the grain markets I prefer, but I can't do that *and* take screenshots, so I will stick to the beans.

The illustration below shows my trading screen at 00:22:56. (All times mentioned in this chapter are given in Queensland time. The market opens at 00:30:00 and closes at 04:15:00. The time format is hh:mm:ss.)

Figure 15.1

SET-UP – SPREADSHEET

You can see the time just above my trading calculator on the right-hand side of the screenshot. I have checked all the values in the bottom portion of the trading calculator are correct. Note how I could get the **Price** and **Change** values from the top line of the chart window. I've set the stop loss level at 0.5 and the profit level at 1.5, as I have in all my examples.

At this stage, the chart being displayed is yesterday's primary session. In about seven minutes, the chart will automatically reset and start tracking today's session. I'm ready to go.

The next shot is taken at 00:32:09.

Figure 15.2

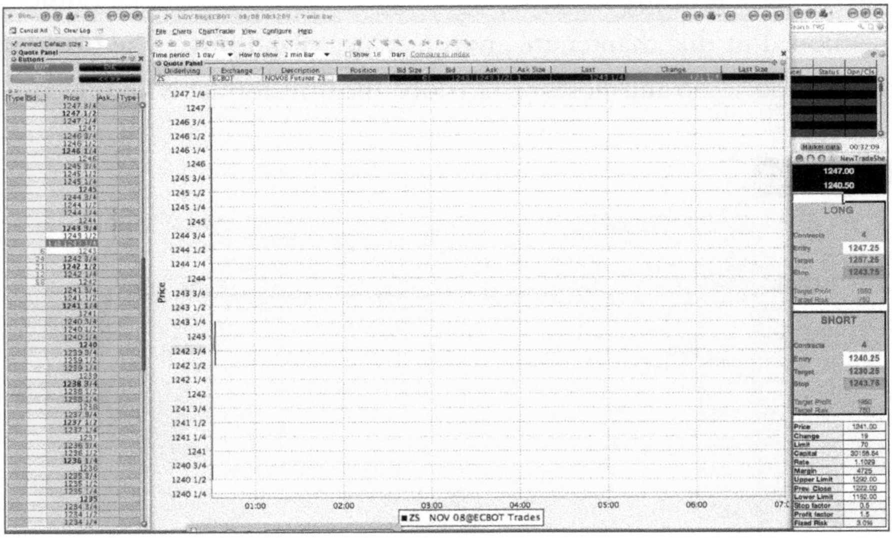

See what I mean about starting the charts with a clean sheet?

So far there is just one completed candle, and the second is just beginning to form. As a matter of technique, I've put the top and bottom values of the first candle into the top two boxes of my trading calculator, because right now they represent the opening range r. From the first blue candle, I take my initial trend as up.

The next shot is taken at 00:34:37.

Figure 15.3

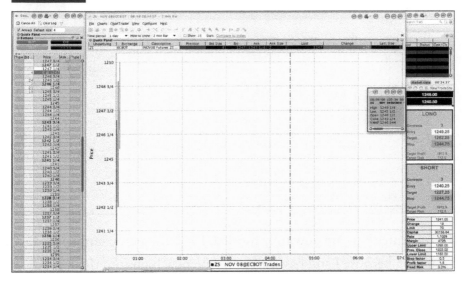

Price is moving steadily up. Two candles have been fully formed and the third is developing. The 2nd box in my trading calculator, representing the lower end of the current opening range, is still at 1240.5, and, as a matter of technique, I'm just keying in new values in the top box as new highs are made. The last value I keyed in was 1249, although I can see from the chart that 1250 has just been touched.

The next shot is taken at 00:36:01.

Figure 15.4

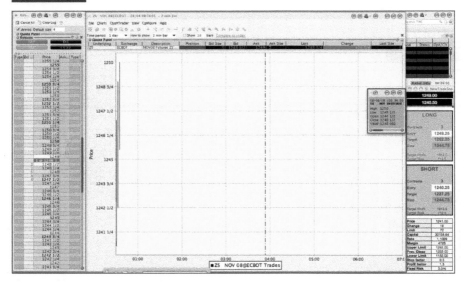

The first three bars are now fully formed. I've been a little tardy with the calculator, because I still haven't put in the new high into the top box.

The next shot is taken at 00:36:25.

Figure 15.5

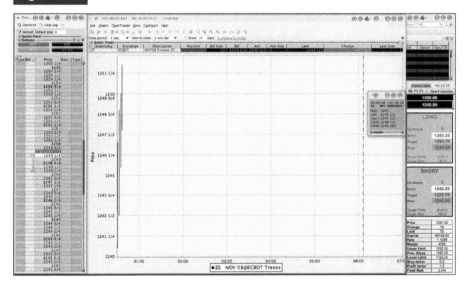

The fourth candle is moving upwards again. I've updated the calculator, but I'll need to do it again as another new high has come in the last few seconds.

The next shot, taken at 00:37:13, shows this latest candle developing. I'm continuing to track the top of the range in the calculator.

Figure 15.6

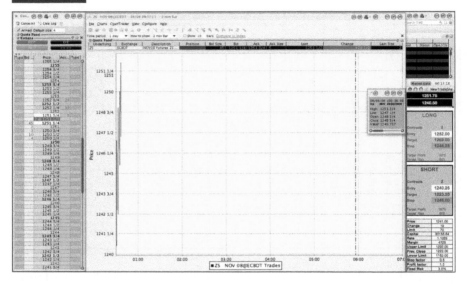

The next shot is taken at 00:39:11.

Figure 15.7

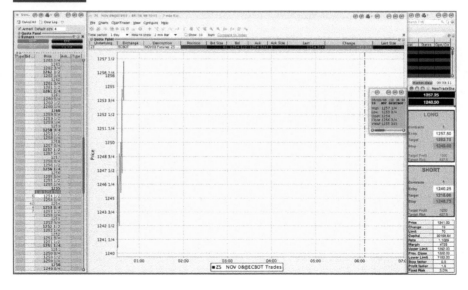

MARKET RISING

The fifth candle is another strong upward move. We've been going nearly ten minutes, and the market is rising strongly. No sign of a pullback yet.

The next two shots, taken at 00:40:54 and 00:41:56 respectively, show the formation of the sixth candle, which is the first pullback candle, because its high is lower than that of the preceding candle.

Figure 15.8

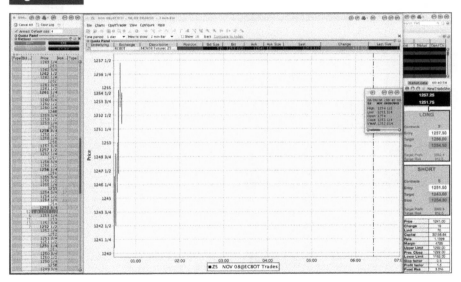

For convenience, let me remind you of my definition of a *pullback* in a rising market:

> **After the market makes a new session high at Point A (resistance level), I define a pullback as occurring if at least 2 consecutive following bars have lower highs than Point A.**

So, in this case the resistance level is established at the top of candle 5 (1257.25). I have one pullback candle, but cannot classify it as a valid pullback until I get a second candle. Notice that the calculator is updated with the top of the range.

Figure 15.9

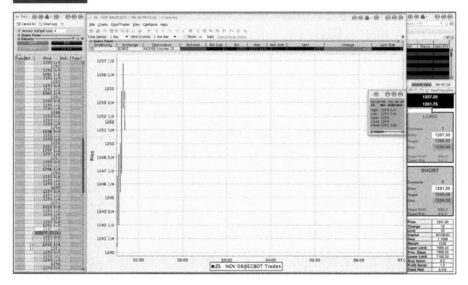

The next two shots, taken at 00:43:49 and 00:44:14 respectively, show the formation of the seventh candle.

Figure 15.10

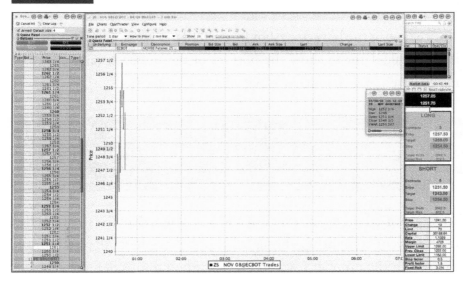

Figure 15.11

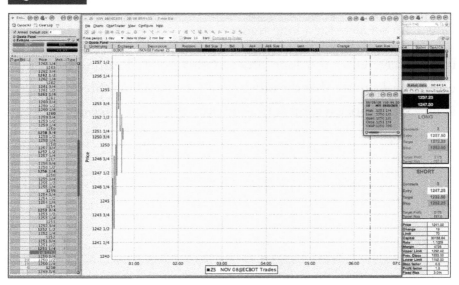

PULLBACK

As its high point is also lower than the resistance level (1257.25), this is confirmation of a pullback, and now if price were to turn up and penetrate resistance I would open a long trade.

Notice how in the last screenshot I have updated the second box in the trading calculator to show the bottom of the pullback range, 1247.5. Here is the range definition I specified in chapter 11.

> **For a long trade, I look back to find the low of the last candle which had a lower low and lower high than its immediately preceding candle.**

The seventh candle has a lower low and lower high than the sixth candle. If price went straight up through Point A from here, the bottom of candle 7 is the number I would use according to this definition.

ON ALERT FOR A LONG TRADE

Now I am on alert for a long trade.

I could have entered a long order at this point. Reading from my calculator, I can see that the order would be to go long three contracts at 1257.50. As price is some way away from this point, I haven't entered the order yet.

The next shot is taken at 00:52:12.

> **Figure 15.12**

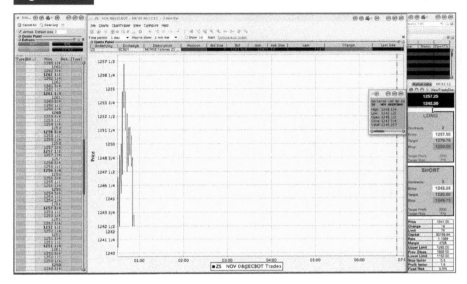

OK, now we have a further strong pullback. The trend is still up, but from the calculator (now updated with the new pullback low of 1242.5) I can see that I would only take two contracts if I did go long above the resistance level.

The next shot is taken at 00:58:03.

Figure 15.13

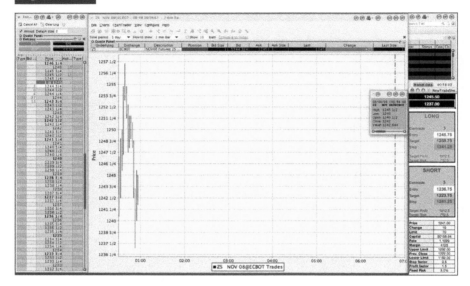

Things have changed!

We have just completed fourteen full bars and are starting on the next. However, candle 12 broke back down through the support level at 1240.50. As explained in an earlier chapter, that means that I change my view of the prevailing trend from up to down, and await a pullback from the new low.

As it happens, candle 13 is a pullback candle, and the pullback is confirmed by candle 14, which also has a higher low than the new support level (1237).

The calculator is now set up showing the range for the short trade. 1237 is the low. 1246.75 is the pullback top. From the calculator I can see that I can enter an order for three contracts to go short at 1236.75.

The next shot is taken at 00:58:26, just a few seconds after the previous one.

Figure 15.14

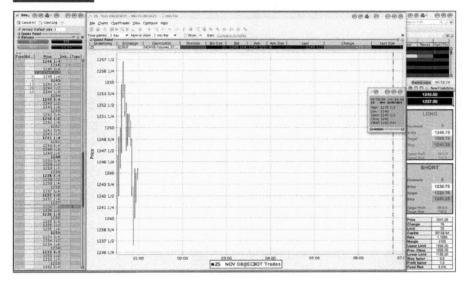

Notice the Book Trader window on the left. With one click, I have entered the stop entry order at 1236.75.

The next shot is taken at 01:00:07, after the first thirty minutes of the trading session have passed.

Figure 15.15

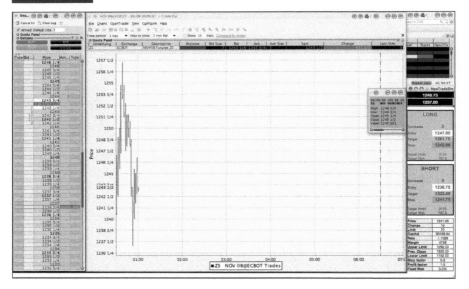

If I don't want to spend too long trading, I close down when I reach this point without entering a trade. But I'll stay on tonight.

The pullback has extended further upwards. I've adjusted the calculator, but don't have to change the order because it is still showing three contracts at the same entry point.

The next shot is taken at 01:04:53.

Figure 15.16

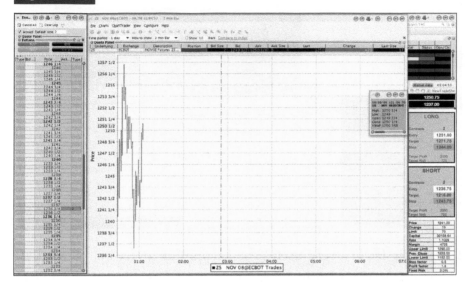

TREND REMAINS DOWN

Now the pullback has really extended way back up. However, the upper resistance level hasn't been penetrated, so the trend remains down. Putting the new top of the pullback range (1250.75) into the calculator shows that I can now only enter two contracts. Notice that I have amended the Book Trader order from three to two contracts.

CHECKING THE ACTION IN THE OTHER GRAINS

This next screenshot taken at 01:05:34 is an interesting diversion. The iMac has a nice facility where, with one key stroke, I can see all the windows that are open. As well as the beans chart, I also have the wheat and corn charts open, although they are normally hidden behind the beans chart. When I press my option key, all the windows become visible like this:

Figure 15.17

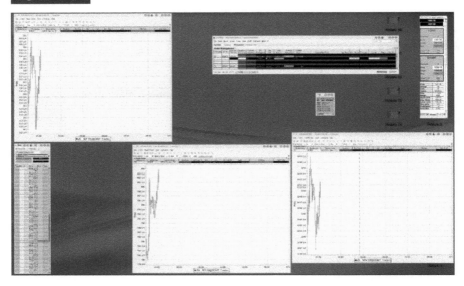

I find this facility very useful for keeping an overview of what is happening in the grain markets. Often, I delay the decision of which market to trade until I can compare the opening action using this view.

My daughter-in-law, who I taught to trade, just messaged me to say she is long the wheat contract. With one key stroke, I have displayed the charts for the three major grain contracts. Corn is the chart on the left, wheat is in the middle, and our beans chart is over on the right.

Wheat started the session trending down, before moving back and penetrating resistance to change the trend to up. It then pulled back from the newly established resistance level, before moving back up and breaking through it, initiating the long trade. On a normal day, I would have monitored these three contracts constantly, and, as I often take the first one to break out, I would probably have been in this trade too if it hadn't been for doing the screenshots. Oh, well! I wish my daughter-in-law good luck, and get back to beans…

The following three screenshots show price drifting back down again, although certainly not getting very close to triggering my stop entry order down at 1236.75.

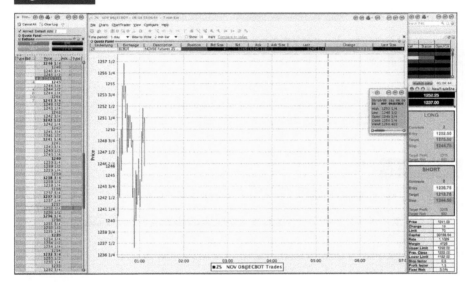

Figure 15.19

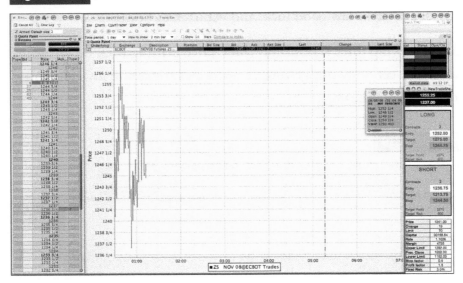

Figure 15.20

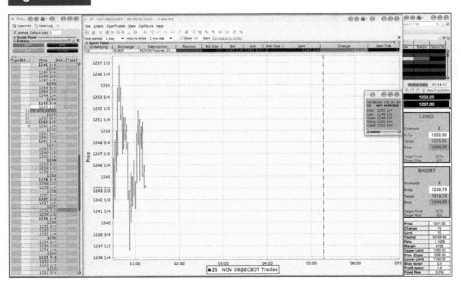

Let's see how my daughter-in-law is getting on at 01:15:27.

Figure 15.21

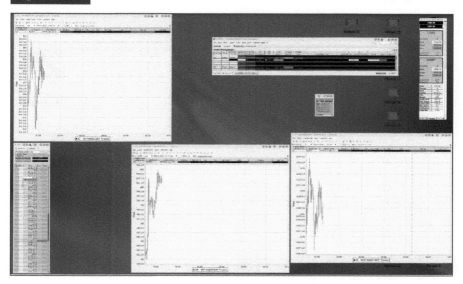

The jury is still very much out on her trade. Price is hanging around in a new trading range near her entry point. I cross my fingers for her.

The next shot is taken at 01:16:30.

Figure 15.22

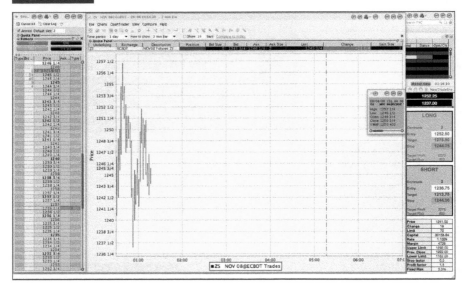

There still isn't much happening for us.

Price is hanging around in the middle of our range, and giving no indication of breaking out anytime soon. It just looks like one of those choppy, non-trending days, but appearances can be deceptive, so it is best to stick with the system.

In the next two screenshots, price is drifting back up a bit.

Figure 15.23

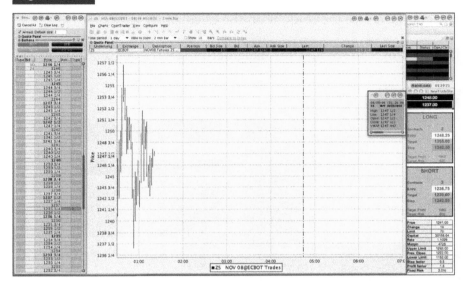

Figure 15.24

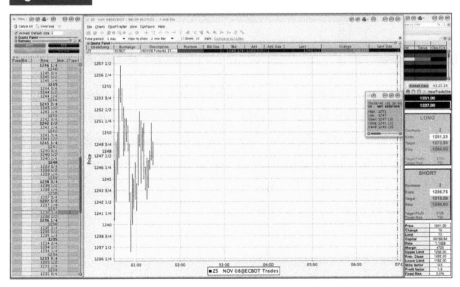

The thing to notice here is that we get a new pullback candle with a higher high and higher low than its preceding candle, so I adjust the top of the range to 1251. It doesn't change the order, which remains for two contracts (see the readout on the calculator).

Let's flick over to see how my daughter-in-law is doing.

Figure 15.25

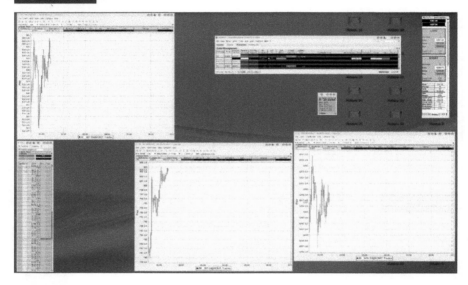

Nowhere near her target yet, but wheat does seem to be holding a stronger tone than beans tonight. Often the two markets move in lockstep, but not tonight. She's sent me a message to say she's put her automatic orders in as an OCA group and taken the new baby with her back to bed. Good! The markets are choppy, and watching them could tempt her to make a rash decision.

The next shot is taken at 01:30:28.

Figure 15.26

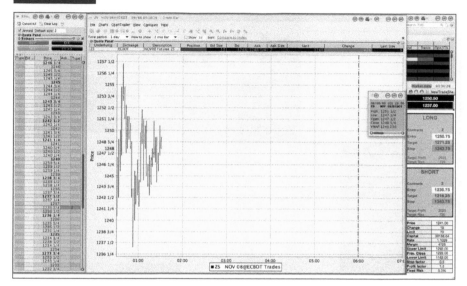

An hour has passed, and still no trade. The beans are looking distinctly uninviting, very choppy. But my job is to implement the system to the best of my ability, and so far so good. After another little move to the upside, I've readjusted the top of the range in the calculator to 1250.5.

I'm going to check on my daughter-in-law's trade, again.

Figure 15.27

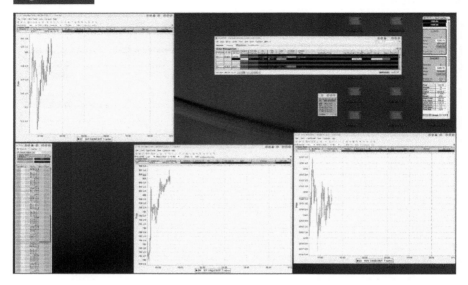

The trade took a spike in the right direction, before plunging back down again. It's still well away from the stop loss, though. I'm glad she isn't watching it.

My next shot is taken at 01:38:31.

Figure 15.28

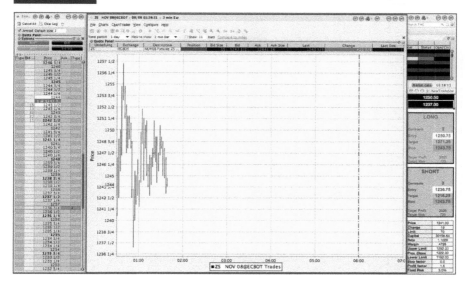

Beans are making another run lower. Still no change to the calculator range or to my stop entry order waiting for a breakout at the bottom of the range.

The next candle shows a strong downward thrust.

Figure 15.29

But then there is another pullback to the upside.

Figure 15.30

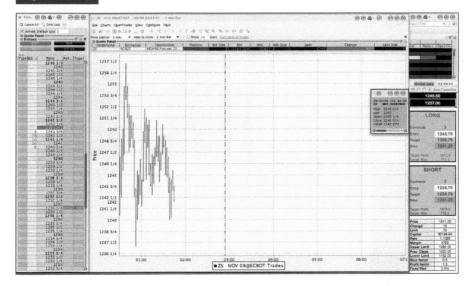

The pullback candle has a higher high and higher low than its predecessor, so I enter the high (1246.75) as the new top of range, in the top box of my calculator. This tells me to change my order to three contracts, which you can see I have done in the Book Trader window.

Oh dear!

My daughter-in-law's trade is looking decidedly sick, although it's still clear of the stop loss. Fortunately she's asleep, and totally unconcerned.

Figure 15.31

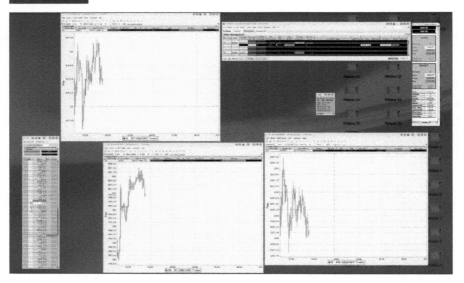

OK. Here we go!

Price has moved straight back down and is seriously challenging the lower limit of the range.

Figure 15.32

Look at the price showing in the Book Trader window in the next screenshot; just one pip above my entry order.

The next shot is taken at 01:50:05.

TRADE EXECUTED

After an hour and fifty minutes, an unusually long time, we are in the trade!

See how the entry order on the Book Trader has clicked down to zero, indicating the order has been filled. There is also a loud "ding" when the order fires.

Note that I've already put in the stop loss at 1241.25. If my system went down now, I would be safe. See how the position field up at the top of the chart window is showing "-3", meaning I am short three contracts? Now is the time for routine and technique. It's tempting to stare at the screen, but there is work to be done…

The first thing I do is scroll down the Book Trader window and, with a single click, enter the profit-taking limit order shown on the calculator at 1223.75. I've also clicked in the top right hand corner of the screen to bring the basic TWS trading window to the front. It is the dark coloured window at the top. Notice how the stop loss and limit orders I entered on the Book Trader window are showing in this window too.

Figure 15.35

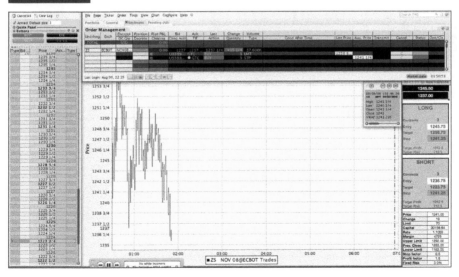

My next task is to re-enter these two orders, together with a market order in case neither of them get hit before the session ends, and link them all into an OCA group.

In the next shot you can see that I have entered three new order lines above the two orders which are already working. The TWS trading software knows they are an OCA group because I have given them a common OCA code ("aaa"). The limit and stop orders are identical to the two already working.

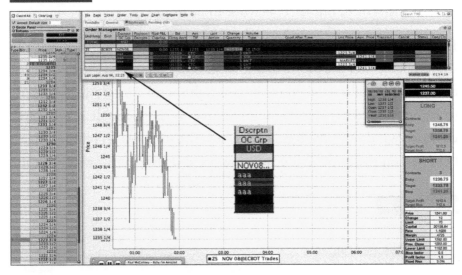

In the next shot, I've cancelled the two existing orders, and transmitted the two identical replacement orders.

Figure 15.37

This might seem a bit complicated, but it is very important.

I originally entered the orders straight away in Book Trader to ensure that my position is immediately protected, and also because the market can move very fast. Sometimes these orders are hit before I even have time to put in the replacement orders! The reason I replace them is that these original orders are not linked in an OCA group. The danger is that they could both be triggered.

For example, the market could move up and trigger the stop loss. This would buy three contracts, cancelling out my short position. But then price could turn down again, triggering the profit taking-limit order, which would also buy 3 contracts. Now, instead of being flat as intended, I'm long three contracts in a falling market!

By linking the orders in an OCA group, this shouldn't happen. When any of the orders, such as the stop loss order, is triggered, the other orders in the OCA group are automatically cancelled, even if you are sleeping peacefully in your bed. That's what we want!

In the next shot, you can see that I am setting up the third order in my OCA group, the Good After Time market order.

Figure 15.38

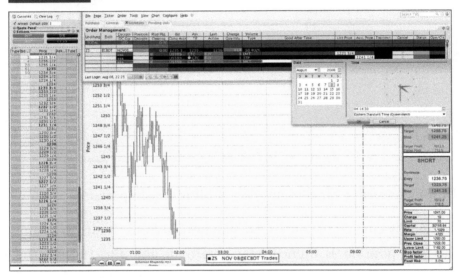

It is possible, although unlikely, that the market will not go up to my stop loss level *or* down to my target level before the end of the session.[5] There is no way I want to be exposed to large potential losses if the market gaps up overnight, so whatever the situation at the close of play today, I want to close the trade. To do this I use the Good After Time option on a normal market order.

---

5   I would set this for five minutes before the end of session now. Orders in the last minute are no longer accepted.

As you can see, I've set up this market order to fire 30 seconds before the end of the session. Of course, the likelihood is it will have been automatically cancelled long before then, but I want to be covered for all eventualities when leaving the trade on autopilot.

The next shot is taken at 02:00:51.

Figure 15.39

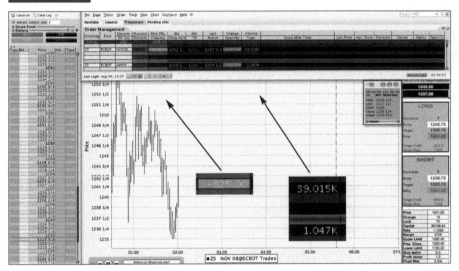

STOP LOSS TRIGGERED

Unfortunately for me, the market has moved up sharply and taken out my stop loss at 1241.25.

The automated orders have worked perfectly. Looking at the TWS window, you can see that the stop loss order closed the position for a loss of $825, and the other two orders in the OCA group were cancelled and no longer show on the screen.

That is a perfect result, insofar as no mistakes have been made and I executed my plan perfectly. The trade turned out to be a loss, but it was handled correctly.

Dealing properly with losses is one of the most important aspects of this business, so I can give myself a pat on the back for this trade. Notice that my calculator predicted a loss of $712.50, and I ended up down $825. That was because the slippage on the second (closing) transaction was bigger than normal tonight. Annoying, but not a tragedy.

CHECKING VOLUME

One small point here.

Notice that on the TWS screen I display two lines for the ZS (soybean) contract. One is for the November contract that I am currently trading, the other is for the January contract, which will be the next contract I move to. The reason I do this is to check the volume. You can see that the volume showing on the November contract was 39.015k, while the January contract had a volume of just 1.04k. Sometime toward the end of October, the volume on the Jan 09 contract will overtake the volume on the Nov 08 contract, and that is when I start trading January instead of November. I always want to be trading the most liquid contract, and I never want to trade a contract in its expiry month.

A LAW OF NATURE

The next screenshot illustrates a mysterious law of nature.

See how price, having taken out my stop, resumed its downward march. This is one of life's great mysteries; you should try not to lose sleep about it. The corollary to this law is that, if you don't take the stop, the market continues to run against you!

Figure 15.40

The market went down even further, although it never did reach my original downside target at 1223.75. The next screenshot shows the completed chart after the session has closed.

Figure 15.41

DE-BRIEFING

What I want to emphasise here is how different it is picking out patterns and potential trades on a completed chart to picking them with the partial picture you have in real-time!

Go back to the first few screenshots. Could you have possibly predicted what the final chart would look like?

I couldn't.

Did all this negativity in the beans market pulldown wheat and spoil my daughter-in-law's trade?

Here's the wheat chart for the completed session.

Figure 15.42

I've shown the trading calculator set up correctly as it was when the trade was entered, and marked the entry, stop loss and target levels on the chart.

The breakout was just after 01:00:00 and, after an initial drift upwards, price came down and flirted with the stop loss line before charging up again strongly. Then it went down again for over an hour, before a final surge near the end of the session took it up through the target level.

So, it ended up a winner, and from the trading calculator I can see that if I had been in this trade I would have made around $1650. (What she made is, of course, dependent on how many contracts she took, which in turn depends on her capital and the setting for the fixed risk percentage.) Anyway, it looks like the family was in the black for the night!

I am prepared to bet that if she had been sitting watching this trade she would not have waited for it to hit her target. Those two big negative moves would have forced her into an early exit as sure as eggs are eggs. You may be sitting there, dear reader, saying, "Not me!", but I can assure you that very few traders do hold on in this situation.

> **Setting up automatic orders in an OCA group and going to bed, or out for a run, is the low stress way of making sure you don't make a sub-optimum decision.**

CHAPTER 16:
A Month at the Tables

T HE PREVIOUS CHAPTER gave us the myopic view of the process. We saw what happens minute-by-minute. Now, let's take a longer view.

As explained in the earlier chapters, I see my business very simply:

1. I place a calculated bet every night, taking every precaution to manage risk as carefully as I am able.

2. I use a simple breakout entry system, which I believe gives me around 55% winners.

3. I aim to have my average win bigger than my average loss.

What I propose to do now is take you through a month of trading.

For simplicity, I will focus on just one market, corn, although often I look at the open before deciding which grain contract to trade. I've chosen April 2008, which was an interesting trading month, although certainly not the best I could have chosen.

Note: this is a simulation, so you should treat it with caution.

Simulated results are usually difficult to achieve in practice. I have assumed the actual win or loss figure will be the target win or loss shown in the trading calculator, less a further $100 for commissions and slippage.

The target figures already have some allowance for slippage built in, so this is a generous allowance. Because corn has the greatest volume and least volatility of the three grain contracts, I often find there is no slippage at all when trading this market.

I've also assumed a margin of $1500 per corn contract for the purposes of this example, and that the trader starts with $25,000 capital.

The contract is traded in a mechanical manner, following the trading rules set out in the earlier chapters to the letter. Some experienced traders may look at some of the decisions and wince, because they can see that the mechanical setup is sometimes a poor one. Occasionally in my own trading I exercise judgement if there is a close call, but my purpose here is to illustrate what can happen if you follow a reasonable plan with strict discipline.

1 APRIL

Figure 16.1

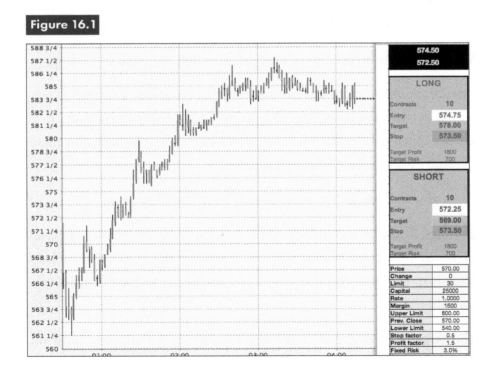

The first candle sets a downward trend bias, and price moves down for the first four candles, before retracing. Eventually resistance at the top of the first candle is penetrated, and the trend bias changes to up (long). After a while, a new resistance level is set and a tight little pullback develops, giving a long trade when price breaks back up through the new resistance level.

You can see the trading range set up in the trading calculator, generating an order for 10 contracts, entry at 574.75, target at 578, and stop at 573.50.

From the chart, it is clear that price moved straight up to the target without approaching the stop loss, so this was a winner. I've assumed that the actual win was $100 less than the $1800 target profit shown in the calculator, so capital on the next trade will be USD26,700.

2 APRIL

Figure 16.2

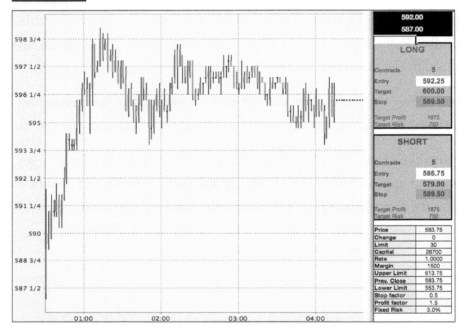

The first candle sets an upward bias. The second candle pulls back, and the pullback persists until resistance is penetrated in the fifth candle, triggering a long trade.

Looking back through the pullback candles (candles 2, 3, and 4), you can see that none of them have a lower high *and* lower low than their preceding candle, so I take the low end of the range as the low for the day (587). This set-up is shown in the trading calculator. It shows 5 contracts, with a target at 600 and stop at 589.50. Neither the stop nor the target is hit during the remaining session, so we exit 30 seconds before the end of the session, when the price is around 596. The target entry was at 592.25.

To be conservative, I've assumed a profit of 3.5 points per contract, 17.5 points in total, or $875. Deducting the standard $100 for costs leaves us with a new capital figure of $27,475.

3 APRIL

Figure 16.3

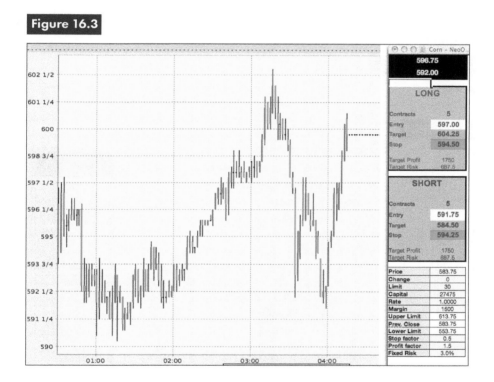

This is the first short trade.

The first candle establishes a downward trend bias, but this is immediately reversed when the second candle moves up. Eventually, though, the negative bias is re-established by the strong move down through support in candle 9. A pullback develops, before a further break downwards right at 01:00 establishes a short trade. The last full pullback candle (with a higher high and higher low than the preceding candle) is candle 6.

The calculator shows a trade for 5 contracts, entering at 591.75, target 584.50, with the stop at 594.25.

You can see from the chart that the trade moves well for quite a while, but price never hits the target, and eventually moves back up to the stop loss level, for a losing trade. The target risk on the calculator is showing $687.5, so I assume a loss of $788, reducing the capital to $26,687.

4 APRIL

Figure 16.4

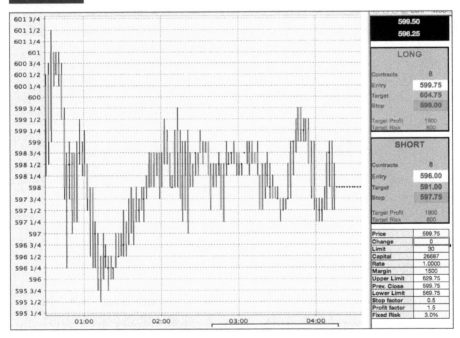

After an upward move, the trend bias switches to down and a pullback develops. Eventually there is a downside breakout, but it goes nowhere, for a loss of 800 + 100 = $900.

7 APRIL

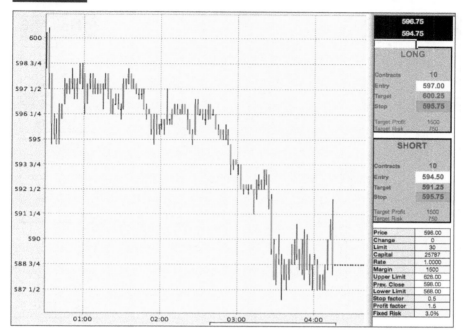

Figure 16.5

It is uncommon in the grain markets for the second candle to be an outside candle, with a higher high and a lower low than the first candle. When this happens, as it did on this day, I disregard the 1st candle completely. The second candle establishes a downward bias, which remains in force a long time before support is eventually penetrated just before 03:00.

You can see from the illustration that the resulting short trade, with a target of 591.25, is a clear winner. Assume a profit of 1500 - 100 = $1400.

8 APRIL

Figure 16.6

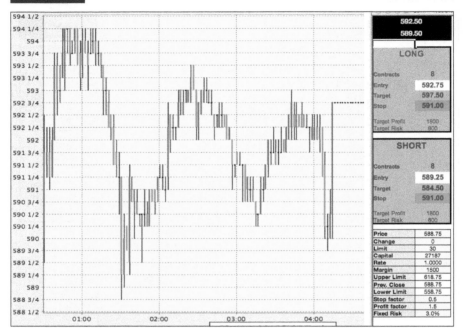

Here is another case where **r** must be set to the full opening range (because none of the pullback bars have a lower high and lower low than their preceding candle).

As can be seen, the resulting trade is a loser ($800 plus $100 costs).

9 APRIL

Figure 16.7

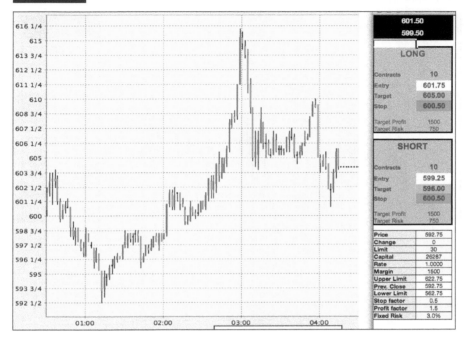

After starting with a long bias, the pullback penetrated support and the trend bias changes to a short trade.

The three-candle pullback sets up a straightforward short trade which nets $1500 profit, less $100 costs.

10 APRIL

Figure 16.8

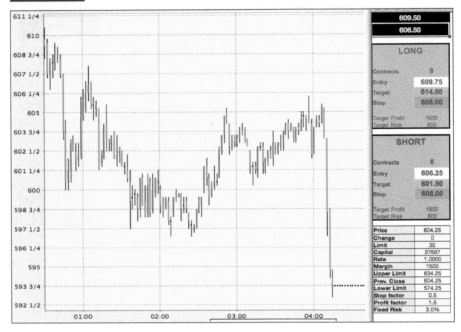

This is a standard short trade.

The market moves down, pulls back, and then breaks downwards for a quick win in less than two bars. Profit is $1800, less $100 costs.

11 APRIL

Figure 16.9

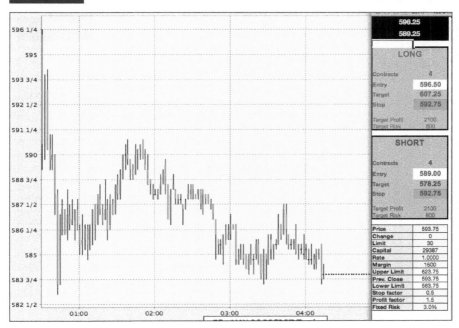

Another standard short trade, but it does not reach the target. Nor does it get stopped out, so we exit 30 seconds before the end of the session at a price around 584. The planned entry was 589 with 5 contracts. To be conservative, assume 4 points profit per contract, 20 points in all ($1000, less $100 costs).

14 APRIL

Figure 16.10

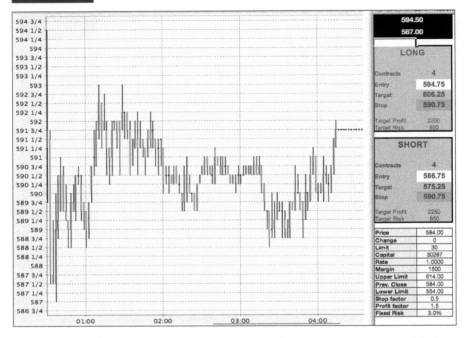

This is a no-trade day, because the broad opening range establishes support and resistance levels that are never breached during the remainder of the session.

15 APRIL

Figure 16.11

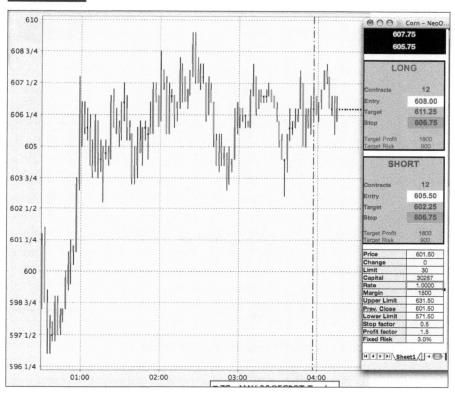

This is a day where the strict application of my entry rules does not work out too well.

After an initial move up, the trend bias changes to short in candle 3, before switching back to long on the 14th candle. As it turns out, that would have been the place to go long, and my actual trade at 02:00 turns out to be a loser ($900 plus $100 costs).

16 APRIL

Figure 16.12

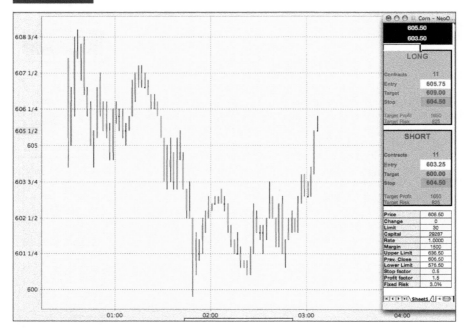

Strict adherence to my rules results in a no-trade day.

A negative bias is established when the market moves down around 01:30, but the subsequent pullback does not contain two consecutive bars with *higher* lows than the current low of the range (603.5).

As a matter of interest, I *did* choose to take the trade shown on this day, but I will not count it here. (Note that I had an internet problem and did not get a complete screenshot of the full session.)

17 APRIL

Figure 16.13

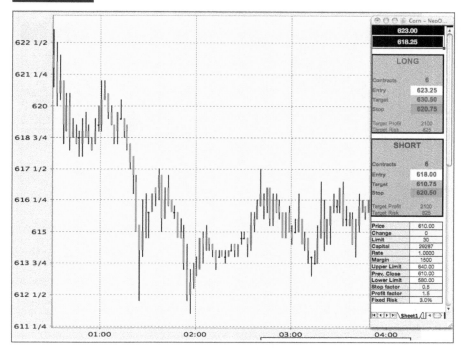

The initial trend bias is short, and there are two separate one candle attempts at a pullback before a small valid pullback finally occurs (candles 7 and 8). Neither is a complete pullback candle, and as there are no earlier complete pullback bars, the upper limit of candle 1 is taken as the top of the range.

Unfortunately, it is clear from the chart that the stop at 620.75 is touched before the trade would have gone on to be an easy winner. The loss is $825 plus $100 costs.

18 APRIL

Figure 16.14

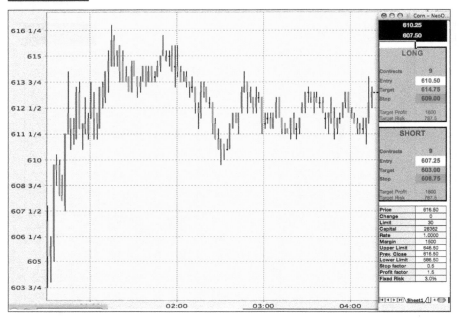

The first candle has a short bias, quickly reversed when the second candle moves up. Candles 5 and 6 pullback from the high before the breakout at candle 7, which gives an easy win. Note that, in this case, the breakout candle has a lower low than either of the other pullback bars.

In a case like this, I usually use the low of the breakout candle as the bottom of my range. This trade makes a profit of $1800, less $100 costs.

21 APRIL

Figure 16.15

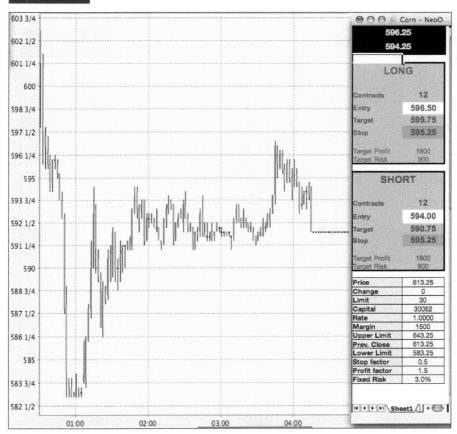

Here is a very quick short trade, all over in the first 25 minutes of the session.

The profit is $1800, less $100 costs.

22 APRIL

Figure 16.16

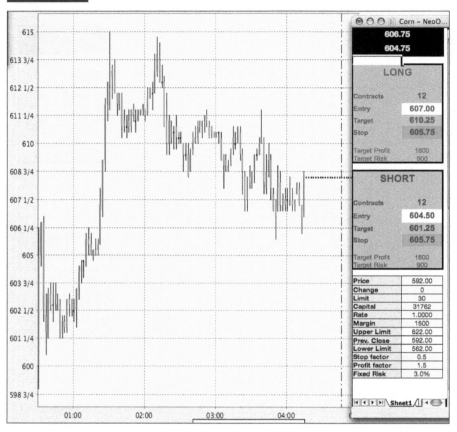

After a strong move up followed by quite a sharp retracement, price eventually breaks up through resistance.

The trade is a clear winner, netting $1800, less costs.

23 APRIL

Figure 16.17

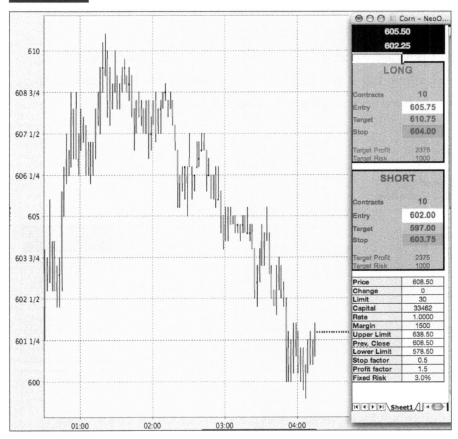

When I went through these examples, I initially missed the fact that this is a third candle breakout. See how the first candle has a long bias, the second candle is a pullback, and the third candle continues upwards? Had I set the calculator up for this trade, with the top of the range at 604 and the bottom at 602.75, I would have had a trade with 21 contracts, target 606.25, and stop 603.6. The trade would have been a loser.

Having missed this, the calculator is set up in the illustration to take the long trade after the pullback during bars 4 to 7. The target is 610.75, and this is just missed as the market doesn't make it above 610.5.

This is a case where a trader watching the trade would be unlikely to take a loss, but if you had automated the exits as I recommend there would have been a full loss ($1000 plus $100 costs).

24 APRIL

Figure 16.18

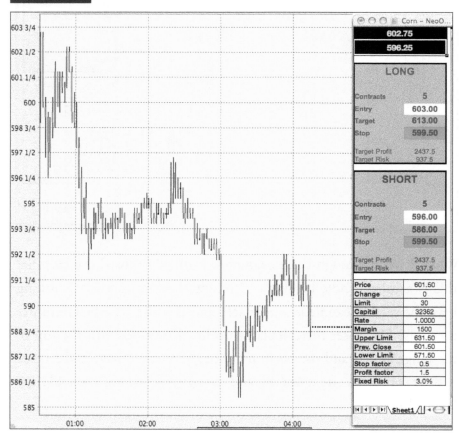

The upward bias set by the first candle is reversed when the second candle moves down. After a deep pullback, the market move penetrates support just after 01:00, eventually just touching the target round about 03:15 for a profit of $2437, less $100 costs.

25 APRIL

Figure 16.19

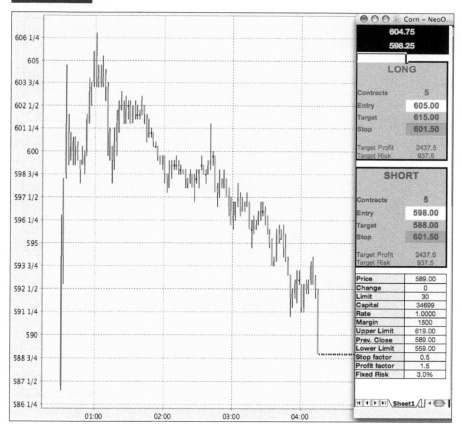

There is a very strong upward move in the first few bars, a pullback, and then an upward breakout. This is an obvious losing trade, and one that many an experienced trader wouldn't enter. Still, keeping faith with the mechanical system, we record a loss of $938, plus $100 costs.

28 APRIL

Figure 16.20

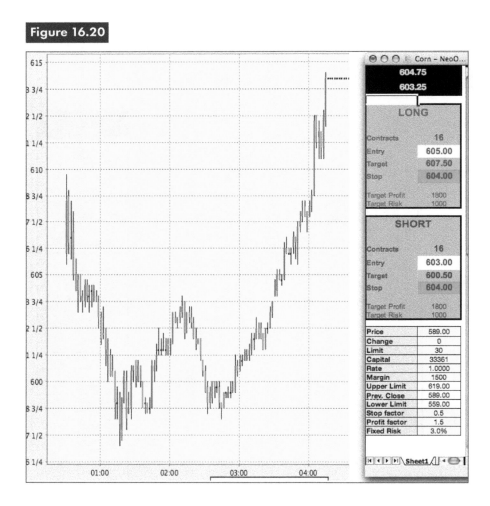

The positive bias set by the first candle is reversed when price moves down through support in candle 6. A new low is established, followed by a shallow pullback, which sets up a winning short trade. Profit is $1800, less $100 costs.

29 APRIL

Figure 16.21

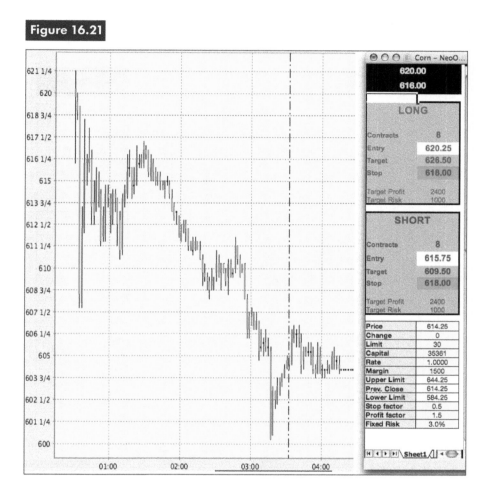

This is a third candle breakout trade on the short side.

The opening candle sets a negative bias, the second candle is a pullback, and the third candle breaks out to the downside. Profit is $2400, less $100 costs.

30 APRIL

Figure 16.22

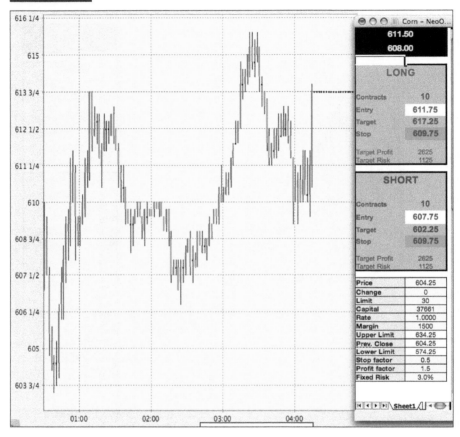

A losing trade to end the month!

Bias moves from long (candle 1) to short (candle 3), and then back to long (candle 12), before establishing a pullback, which is followed by a breakout. The stop is hit for a loss of $1125, plus $100 costs.

Month's trading summary

Figure 16.23

611.50	
608.00	

LONG

Contracts	9
Entry	611.75
Target	617.25
Stop	609.75
Target Profit	2362.5
Target Risk	1012.5

SHORT

Contracts	9
Entry	607.75
Target	602.25
Stop	609.75
Target Profit	2362.5
Target Risk	1012.5

Price	613.75
Change	0
Limit	30
Capital	36436
Rate	1.0000
Margin	1500
Upper Limit	643.75
Prev. Close	613.75
Lower Limit	583.75
Stop factor	0.5
Profit factor	1.5
Fixed Risk	3.0%

The final shot shows the trade calculator as we move into May.

The trade capital has increased from $25,000 to $36,436, which is a good result in anybody's language. As I said earlier, simulated results are hard to achieve in practice. But even if you made some errors, halving your returns, this is still a good month.

Notice how quickly the compounding effect is occurring, assuming wins are left in the trading account where they add to the trading capital for the next trade. This is the benefit of leverage combined with prudent money management.

Reviewing the statistics for the month, we see that out of 22 trades, there were 12 winners, 8 losers and 2 no-trades. That means the probability of a win was 12 out of 20 (60%). The average win was $1709 and the average loss was $884.5, giving a win to loss ratio of 1.93. I traded on 20 out of 22 days (91%).

In chapter 4, I set down the guidelines I like my trading system to meet each month. To recap:

- I aim to be using a strategy with a 50% (or better) chance of winning,
- where my (actual) average win is substantially bigger than my average loss, and
- I get to trade in at least 80% of all sessions.

Over time, the most difficult statistic for me to keep right is the percentage of wins. However, even if it drops to 40% in a particular month, I'm still ahead as long as my win to loss ratio stays at about two.

This month easily met the guidelines.

CHAPTER 17:
The Importance of Practice

NOBODY EVER GOT to be excellent at anything without practice. Trading, and particularly high speed day trading, is no exception.

The trickiest part of my system is:

- recognising support and resistance levels
- correctly identifying pullbacks
- identifying the range, r.

The best way of learning to do this instinctively is to study chart after chart. Even now, after years of trading, I spend time each day looking at old charts and identifying how they should have been traded.

If you practice enough, the pattern recognition becomes second nature, and you begin to feel as though you are "in the zone" when you trade. Not only can you recognise formed patterns after they occur, but you find yourself anticipating the likely formation of patterns before they occur.

To the beginner, a chart is a jumble of candlesticks with no clear form, but after a while you reach a stage where you can pick trading opportunities with one quick glance.

LIBRARY OF HISTORIC CHARTS

A problem you might have is finding enough charts to practise on. It is easy enough to find long-term end of day data on the internet, but it is not so easy to find intraday historical two-minute charts for futures contracts.

I solve this problem by taking a screenshot of each of the wheat, corn and soybean two-minute trading charts at the end of each primary session. I keep a library of these, with the result that I now have years of chart data which I can easily access for practice. It's also very useful if I get a bright idea for trading differently. I can quickly see how the idea would have worked out in practice over a long period.

The cost of mistakes

One final word about practice.

Given the probability of winning, the size of an average win and the size of an average loss, it is possible to calculate the *theoretical average profit per trade*, P, for your trading system.

If you know P, you can predict your earnings over many trades:

```
earnings = (number of trades × P) - commissions - slippage
```

Alas, the equation in the real world is as follows:

```
earnings = (number of trades × P) - commissions - slippage
- cost of mistakes!
```

Unfortunately, that last element can be very substantial.

I don't care who you are, when you come to reckon how you did in a particular month, you will find you were less than optimum because you made some errors.

The way to ensure the mistakes element is as small as possible is to practise.

It's not as though a trader's working hours are unduly onerous, so spend a little extra time reviewing charts. It is a solid gold investment of your time.

CHAPTER 18:
The Computer Set-up

B ACK IN CHAPTER 5, I talked about managing risk. This chapter looks at some of the physical factors that are within your control.

A BIG screen!

I trade with an Apple iMac computer that has a 20-inch screen. My next upgrade will be to the 27-inch model. There is a great deal of information to be monitored and you want to see as much of it as you can. If you start trading using a laptop, or a small screen, you are handicapping yourself.

This might seem like a small point, but it's one of those things that you just have to experience. The difference is like chalk and cheese.

The good news is that the screen is the only item of equipment where you need to spend a bit of money. Your PC doesn't need to be super-fast, have extra memory, massive hard drives, high-end graphics cards or any other fancy features. A standard machine with a reliable broadband internet connection is all you need.

When computers crash...

It does pay to have a second computer you can use at a pinch. Computers don't often fail, but if you do have a crash at a critical moment you will be greatly relieved if you can get your system up on an alternative machine.

In case of emergency, make sure you have the phone number of your broker handy and written down – not in the address book on your computer that you can't access if it crashes! If the worst comes to the worst you can ring the broker, check the status of your trade, and enter or cancel orders over the phone.

Make sure your broker offers this service and answers the phone when called!

Internet precautions

About backup, my experience is that broadband internet failures are more common than computer hardware failures. Losing the internet is just as devastating to your trading as a computer hardware failure, and having a spare computer available won't help. Again, be prepared to ring your broker as a last resort. But it is also an excellent idea to have a backup internet connection service.

My backup is a low cost dial-up account with an alternative Internet Service Provider (ISP). I have resorted to this facility from time to time, and it has proved to be a very worthwhile investment.

If you hate dial-up, another alternative that is becoming viable now is a 3G wireless broadband connection. You don't need a plan with much download capacity if it's just for backup.

One more thing: modems fail too. I expect many readers will have a cable or ADSL wireless modem serving two or more computers in the home. If you have one, I recommend that you keep an old modem that you can plug directly into your phone line, just in case that wireless modem fails.

Naturally, all your electronic equipment should be plugged into proper power boards with surge protection, especially if you get the occasional thunderstorm.

Just common sense really.

Backup procedures

These equipment problems happen infrequently. That's where practice and, if you need it, good documentation comes in, because when something happens it might be months since you set up your backup procedures. Questions you should ask include:

- Where did you write down the broker's phone number, with your account number and any other information you need to identify yourself over the phone?

- Is your backup modem configured with the right password so that you can just plug in and go? (There will be no time to listen to the call centre music if you must call your ISP for help getting it set up.)

- Have you kept your backup computer up to date with the latest version of your broker's software?

- Have you remembered to store the latest version of your own tools, like the trading calculator, on your backup machine?

The objective, when the worst comes to the worst, is to be back up and running within minutes. Even then you will find you've doubled your heart rate!

The best thing you can do is practise your procedures by getting the system up, out of hours, and simulating various kinds of problems. Sort out the little things.

> I once had a problem where I needed to switch to dial-up and I couldn't find the telephone lead. I found another one, but it was too short! Take it from me, frantically shifting furniture in the middle of the night, hoping fervently that an unprotected position isn't going against you, is not a good thing.

This business is all about taking calculated, substantial risk to realise big profits. When you enter a trade, you must take a risk. But why take unnecessary risks where your equipment is concerned? How much does it cost these days for a spare PC, a spare modem, and a cheap alternative internet connection? With a bit of planning, and not too much investment, you can virtually eliminate equipment failure and most connectivity risks, so do it!

And don't forget the BIG SCREEN, it will make all the difference.

Logout check list

This might seem like a very mundane item indeed, and it isn't specifically related to the physical computer setup, but after many years of trading I have become quite paranoid about how I log off from the trading platform.

Just as I have a checklist I go through before the trading session opens to ensure all the information in my trading calculator is correct, I have a similar checklist for when I log off:

1. I check my portfolio to verify that it is showing no open positions. I'm a day trader – I want no open positions when I close.

2. I check that there are no pending orders.

3. To be doubly sure, I execute the "cancel all orders" command.

4. Once again, I check that there are no open positions showing for my account.

Only then do I close my trading screens.

All this might seem like overkill. Indeed, if everything has been done to plan, there should be no need for all this caution. However, every now and again things will not have gone entirely to plan. You were rushed and made a mistake perhaps?

It is at these times that you may find an uncancelled order sitting in the system, which you have completely forgotten about. Or perhaps you think you have closed your position, but find that it is still open for some reason. Maybe you were long four contracts, and in a flurry of confusion only closed two of them, leaving the other two active by mistake. These things happen every now and then, and it is distressing to log in the following day and find yourself in an unplanned trade that has notched up substantial losses.

For your own safety, develop a "belts and braces" safety routine for exiting the system, and work through it without fail every time you log off. Think of yourself as being like the pilot performing checks before taking off or landing a jumbo jet.

CHAPTER 19:
The Trading Ritual

T HAT LAST ITEM in the preceding character typifies a lot of what I've learned about trading.

THE SEARCH FOR THE HOLY GRAIL

When I first started in this business, I thought it was all about knowledge and research. I kept abreast of every development in world markets, combed through trading literature and the internet looking for better trading methods, and spent days analysing historical data in spreadsheets, searching for new trading indicators and systems.

My friends were impressed, but despite all this knowledge I wasn't making money.

SIMPLICITY IS THE KEY

It was only after all this chasing that it slowly dawned on me that trading success could be based on the three tried and true concepts of:

1. support and resistance

2. trading with the trend

3. letting winners run while cutting losses quickly.

It's easy to skim quickly over these concepts.

They are so simple.

Almost everyone who has traded knows about them and can tell you what they are. But that doesn't mean they truly appreciate their importance.

It pays to keep the trading process simple. (At least, complexity never worked for me.) The trading style presented in this book is not sophisticated, but it is nevertheless built from strong bricks.

RITUAL AND ROUTINE

> Nowadays, I believe that my success is determined by how well I implement my plan. Trading is the constant repetition of a relatively simple process, striving for perfect implementation. It is a case of doing the same, simple things really well, day after day after day.

Much of this becomes ritual. Just as a pro tennis player might always follow the same routine before serving, a successful trader builds a series of rituals and routines into the day's work. Rituals ensure that we follow a standard process without variation, and help us avoid forgetting something important.

Reducing the trading process to a ritual, which I can perform effortlessly with skill and grace, is the nearest thing to the Holy Grail I've found.

PART II:
Reflections 10 Years On

While reviewing this book to bring it up to date, I thought the reader might be interested in some thoughts from an old trader. If you've got this far, you've read all you need to understand my basic trading technique. This core technique continues to underpin all my trading strategies.

These new chapters talk about lifestyle, attitude and psychology. Boring stuff, I know, and I wouldn't blame you for taking a rain check at this point! Still, somebody may be interested...

CHAPTER 20:
A Winter's Day

I WROTE THE FOLLOWING journal entry at the end of a crisp June day in 2016.

"Today has been perfect. We don't always appreciate perfection at the time. Sometimes we must cast our minds back to remember distant hopes and dreams of yesteryear, and then make a conscious effort to compare the here and now against them. And it's deceptive. When I look back at earlier periods in my life which, in retrospect, were magnificent, I remember them being hard at the time – they didn't feel perfect then!

Conversely, there were times when I thought I'd finally achieved some grand ambition, yet I can scarcely remember those years now. If I had to differentiate, the best times were when I was physically fit, active and striving to improve my strength, endurance or speed; when I was mentally challenged with a project that required intense self-education, was frustrating and difficult, and consumed my spare thoughts; when I was independent to do as I please and my successes and failures were 100% mine and mine alone; when I was a quiet part of my family in tune with its vibrations.

The faded years belong to times when I felt important in my lofty roles, but let my body get round and softened by business lunches and airline schedules; when the projects I undertook were not mine and didn't make my mind soar; when results were less dependent on intellectual application and hard work than they were on political manipulation, networking and cosying up to the right mentor; when successes had a thousand fathers and failure was an orphan; when my life was out of sync and discordant with family.

A perfect life isn't about having lots of money and not having to work, it's about having responsibilities you are fulfilling, challenges you are rising to, dreams you aspire to, hope and optimism in your heart.

When I was a boy in Manchester, walking a dark, slushy path over the golf course, crossing a bridge over the weedy water of a canal with the surface barely visible through bicycle frames, old prams and trolleys, bordered by the semi-derelict bodies of defunct cotton mills, continuing through grey ranks of closely packed terraced houses with front doors opening direct on to the pavement, catching a double decker bus with strands of nicotine dangling from the yellow-stained ceiling of the upper deck, I would dream of one day living in a place where it was warm, with golden beaches, mountains, very few people and exotic wildlife. And yet, and yet… it was a good life.

I am eternally grateful for the wonderful education I enjoyed after passing the eleven-plus exam which enabled a very few kids from my neighbourhood to go to a grammar school. I am grateful to my father who ferried me and others around the country (in a very old A35 van) to camping weekends on the banks of rapid rivers to compete in canoe slaloms. I am grateful that my first employer, IBM, had the vision to sponsor a new department of computer science at my university and paid for a group of us to be the first students to study that novel subject, and then offered us full-time employment. (What a life-changing moment when I opened the *Sunday Times* colour supplement one morning and saw IBM's advertisement for "data processing" students, and decided to abandon university offers to study microbiology in favour of this technology which people said would be the wave of the future!)

But I never lost that vision of a remote land of sun, sand, mountains, wild animals and solitude… I would read travel books and pore over world atlases to find my ideal destination. Would it be Canada, Australia, New Zealand or Brazil? The world was bigger then. Once you had gone, there was no Skype, no email, no photos in the cloud. A phone call cost a small fortune, and really the only practical form of communication was a hand-written letter on flimsy blue airmail paper. Eventually, in my mid-20s, the location question answered itself in the form of a job offer in Wellington, New Zealand, with relocation expenses for my young family.

New Zealand has it all: snow-capped volcanoes, uncrowded sandy beaches, extraordinary seascapes, sailing, skiing, world-best trout fishing in crystal clear rivers and idyllic bush-clad lakes, thermal fields with hot-water geysers, underground rivers – all within a few hours' drive of each other. There are no indigenous mammals, although it has its fair share of imported fauna – deer, goats and wild pigs for example. Did I mention a population of under five million, and a relaxed lifestyle?

I spent 30 years in New Zealand, living briefly in the cities Wellington and Auckland, but mostly in smaller centres like the exotic Bay of Islands in the far north, or the glorious Bay of Plenty on the east coast of the North Island, working in both academic and business life. Only then did I relocate to my third country, Australia, settling on the beautiful Gold Coast in Queensland, with its splendid wildlife and breath-taking beaches, its dense rain forests and bustling cities.

One of my favourite authors, James Lee Burke, writes detective stories based in the small towns of Louisiana around New Orleans, made compelling by Burke's connection with the environment, the sudden rain squalls and violent electrical storms, the gentle rain dimpling the bayou, the suffocating heat and humidity which you feel as if you were there... Well, I often feel he would be at home in Queensland, another big, wild climate with long periods of delightful weather interspersed with some of the heaviest rains, strongest winds, biggest floods and wildest forest fires found anywhere on earth. My son and I love sitting on our deck during summer thunderstorms watching massive lightning forks light up the sky, with bone-shaking thunderclaps rocking the house to its foundations, or watching the eerie sight of thousands of fruit bats flying silently inland as darkness falls.

Today, I woke half an hour before dawn, and, as usual, checked the computer screen for the overnight trading results. (Overnight for me is the previous daytime in Chicago where my trades are done.) For several years now, my trading has been handled by a smart software product[6] I purpose-built for the job, which automates the entire process. I set up a trading plan and leave the software to implement it while I sleep – no more staying up most of the night watching price charts on the screen, looking for trade signals and struggling to take fast, timely action when the right moment arrives...

Anyway, good news, this morning! A win ($2,485) to start the day. As I emphasise in my book, it would have been no big deal if it had been a loss, but even in my 17th trading year, it still lifts the spirits to score a win. Half an hour later, I met my friend down at

---

6   TradeOnAUTO (**www.tradeonauto.com**)

the seafront on Burleigh beach and we ran through the National Park over the headland to Talebudgerra Creek. The waves looked great, so after coffee and a catch-up I headed home, put my stand-up paddle board into the car, and drove to Currumbin.

Surfing is a sport I started a couple of years back, but wish I'd started 50 years ago. There were some guys I know on the sea out there; the waves were glassy and the sun was glinting on the clear water. You get long rides at Currumbin and clear winter days like this with a smaller swell are perfect for my skill level. At one point, we all stopped to watch a big humpback whale repeatedly breaching about a kilometre off shore, a magnificent site. More coffee, then home for lunch and walk the dog around the woods. Even though we are in an urban area, there is a lake and wetlands reserve at our doorstep, and we saw a couple of kangaroos, a sleeping pair of frogmouths, a flock of ibis and a pair of stately great egrets.

Time for some work. Since I wrote TradeOnAUTO a few years back, the programming landscape has changed a lot. Everything still works, but if I am to implement some of the new ideas which have popped into my mind, I need to update my skills. So, for the last several months, I've been studying the latest developments in the Java programming language, examining the updated features in my broker's application programming interface, and thinking how my software can be redesigned to make it even better.

To try it all out, I'm building a client administration tool for my own use, which does all the stuff required to simplify supporting people who have bought the software. It's going well – nearly finished! There are just a few more features I want to build in, even though it's already very workable. So, I spent an enjoyable couple of hours developing and testing some code. When this tool is finished, I'll be ready for the big job – building a new version of TradeOnAUTO. Frankly, I can't wait!

This is exactly what I mean about having a project that fires your enthusiasm, challenges your intellect, is 100% your own idea, and for which you, and only you, are accountable. When the new version is ready to go, it will give me the research tools I need to take my trading to the next level and provide a great upgrade for my software clients.

I'm feeling very energised by all this! A few years ago, I had an accident and lost fingers on my right hand (I'm right-handed) along with various other injuries. As a touch typist, that was a significant injury, and rather took away my enthusiasm for writing, blogging and software development. Apart from servicing existing clients, I just focused on my personal trading for the next few years. But now, completely recovered, it's time to get back into it! There's no time limit, but I plan to spend at least two hours coding most days, until it's done. That fits in well with my other activities, household duties and spending as much time as possible with my wife and son.

Now, almost a year later, I can tell you the new software was completed sooner than I expected, and has enabled me to come up with some very profitable strategies.

This journal entry reflects how trading enabled me to realise dreams, while enjoying a great lifestyle. It's not the money I've made – I might have made more opening a McDonald's franchise – but it's the challenge, freedom, and self-determination that I value most.

CHAPTER 21:
I'm a Trader

My name is David, and I'm a trader!

MAKES ME SOUND like an addict, doesn't it? Well, I am, kind of… In the sense that I hate it when I can't do it; eagerly look forward to my next session; tend to erase previous bad experiences from my mind; and spend a lot of time thinking about it.

For the first few years of my trading career, I was shy about it. I was in my early 50s, had done well in my corporate career, and had just taken an attractive redundancy payment. I felt that, with my natural talent, I should have no trouble putting my capital to work to earn a fine living as a trader. I envisaged a lifestyle in which I moved around the world's exotic places, doing a few minutes trading each morning, and spending the profits during the remainder of the sun-drenched days.

Fortunately, I resisted the urge to tell people about these dreams, simply announcing to friends that I'd retired. As a rule, I didn't even tell them I was trading, because I didn't feel as though I knew enough about it yet. Clearly, I was right! My results were all over the place, but exhibited an undeniable downward trend. I don't see how you can ever be thought of, or think of yourself, as an "expert" trader if you don't consistently make money yourself – yet in this business plenty of people do just that.

So, I studied hard, worked hard, tried everything, built computer models and ran simulations. Not only that, but I consumed every financial journal, every online newsletter, every trading textbook and every real-time business TV channel. I was a walking trading encyclopaedia. I was the go-to man if you needed to know the projected coffee harvest in Brazil, forex trends, all the financial tittle-tattle in the business press, how various fancy option strategies worked, what was up and what was down. All of which meant I could impress people at a BBQ – investment knowledge seems to be something that has a certain mystique – but unfortunately my overall trading results remained firmly stuck in the red.

Nowadays, things are different. When people find out that I'm a trader, they invariably ask my opinion about the current financial situation, or give me their take on what's happening. And, just as it was in those early days, it's a bit embarrassing, but for a different reason. Because, now, I must confess that I haven't a clue!

> "No, I don't know how low the iron ore price can go? Down a bit, is it?"

You see, as I travelled my trading road, I learned that much of what I'd thought important when I started out, had no influence on my results. So now I don't impress anybody – but I do make money trading. That's because I learned to think as a trader rather than as a financial know-it-all. Don't get me wrong, it's probably quite a good idea to familiarise yourself with all that stuff. Just don't expect it to make you a successful trader.

Trading is a zero-sum game. If I win, I take money off other traders, and when they win, I lose. It's not even zero-sum, because there are trading costs. In fact, there is a whole industry of exchanges, brokers, advisors – and we traders need to pay their salaries and send their kids to private schools, before we can even start taking money off each other!

Now, I'm prepared to concede that you, dear reader, being a very smart person who has had a stellar career in some profession or other, may, possibly, take a look at trading and develop an exotic strategy which no one else has ever thought of, and make a gazillion dollars. It's possible, but it's bloody unlikely! However, you are certainly most welcome to think that way and have a go, because it is you and the legions of like-minded people out there who flush through the markets each year and contribute their trading accounts to us old-timers!

The best traders I know don't make money through their in-depth financial expertise. The most profitable market knowledge is "insider" knowledge, and it is illegal to use that (and it's hard to come by anyway!), or "early knowledge" that gets to you legitimately before the rest of the market knows about it. Good luck to you if you think you can get in ahead of the traders attached to big banks and commodity trading companies. Personally, I don't have the contacts, or the internet speed, to hear about market-moving events before you! And my Mac can't compete with the massive computing power built into the high-frequency trading systems deployed by our opposition in the market place. Those whippet-smart young genius traders, employed straight out of university by banks, get all the best trading weapons!

No, I'm a trader. If you are a trader, too, I want your money!

Reading a Wall Street report on why prices moved yesterday ('traders took profits', 'traders were nervous about Chinese trade figures', 'traders bought on expectation of a rate cut') is no earthly use to me. I just want to figure out a way of getting your money in the next few hours. This isn't done by listening to "talking heads", taking advice from others, doing what others are doing, or dithering.

Traders make up their own minds, act decisively, and take responsibility for their decisions – win or lose. That's not to say they just hang round with no clear plan, relying on fast reactions and finely honed instincts – some may, but the majority prefer clear plans to help recognise and exploit opportunities. I am a trader, not a financial guru, not an expert economist, not an accountant. My job isn't to know stuff and predict the future. My job is to outsmart you and (legally) divest you of your wealth.

My favourite game is *Go*. It's an ancient Asian board game played on a board marked up with a matrix of intersecting lines. There are two players, one with a bowl of black stones, the other with a bowl of white stones. At each turn, a player places a stone on the board with the objective of surrounding more territory than his or her opponent, without getting captured in the attempt. The rules are very simple, yet the strategy takes a lifetime to master. In my opinion, it is a richer game than chess.

The point is that a beginner seeks to win every battle, surround all the territory and capture every stone, but this is not possible against a good player. A master understands that to win, it is only necessary to surround one more territory point than the opponent. A local battle can be abandoned if necessary, and territory can be given up for strategic gain. Losses on one part of the board can be offset by gains elsewhere; if you don't fight to the death in a losing battle, you can recoup elsewhere and still win the war!

That's trading.

You can't win every trade. Only a rank amateur would think you could. Every time you lose, you'll probably be upset, but if you can't learn to get over it, don't be a trader. You must expect to lose, and handle those losses strategically, abandoning losing positions quickly to develop winning positions elsewhere. To succeed, "all" you must do is win more than you lose. All the short-term trading tactics you deploy are geared to this overarching truth. Don't get so absorbed in them that you lose sight of the bigger picture. Don't win battles and lose wars.

CHAPTER 22:
What's This Psychology Stuff?

OKAY, I KNOW I promised not to get into psychology, but I couldn't resist! You're right, I'm not a psychologist and I have no credentials in that field. So, take my comments with a grain of salt. Treat them as the random musings of an old trader who has managed to survive as a futures day trader for nearly two decades. Nothing more.

Why do long-term traders harp on about psychology in trading? It's not about that, is it? Surely it's about smarts, skills, market knowledge, analysis? Of course it is, who could deny it?

Just one thing, though... Successfully deploying your talents in fast-paced, cut-throat markets requires discipline, courage, persistence, resilience, and sound judgement. Well, you knew that, didn't you? It's kind of... obvious. You didn't read this far to hear about self-evident stuff. You're here to see if you can pick up a revolutionary new entry signal, find a better market to trade, or examine a clever money management approach.

But here's the thing. I've seen a lot of traders fail, and, let me tell you, very few of them go down because of poor technical skills. No, they lose through lack of discipline and resolve, brought on by fear and panic. So maybe there is something to this psychological stuff, no matter how aggravating it is for the rookie to "waste time" reading about it.

I'll give you a common example. If I show you a back-tested strategy that made an average 75% per year over five years, I dare say you'd think that was pretty good. Suppose it has two or three dips where there is a 15–20% drawdown. Most novices will look right past those drawdowns and focus on the outcome. Of course, you would! When you know the ultimate outcome is positive, what does a 20% drawdown matter?

But the problem is that in real life you *don't* know. I've seen people walk away from trading because they've hit a 10% drawdown. If you have a $100,000 account, it is demoralising when it runs down to $90,000, even though that might be totally expected in your trading strategy. Doubt begins to gnaw your entrails. Has this strategy gone off? Will it come back? After all, whatever the maximum drawdown was in the past, there's almost certainly going to be a deeper one in the future! Hello, sleepless nights.

If anxiety and fear don't make you close your trading account directly in favour of safer activities (like base jumping), you will likely devote hours to further analysis of your strategy. You may conclude that a few minor tweaks will eliminate most of the recent losses, or you might even decide to try that fancy new options technique you've just been reading about. Alternatively, you could harden up and stick with your strategy to the bitter end, going down with all guns blazing.

Any one of these decisions could be a master stroke, or a complete dud, and there is *no way of knowing in advance*. That is what makes trading stressful and it is why the great majority of people can't do it. Many aspiring traders walk away from a perfectly good strategy at the lowest point of their first significant drawdown, maximising their loss, only to see results soar to new highs with them no longer aboard. Or they constantly "curve fit" the strategy by adding new rules and filters which would have saved them from recent losses, only to see those same new rules and filters sabotage the strategy in the future! Sometimes they become gun-shy and search desperately for a strategy that has few losses and a lot of wins – like, for instance, selling way-out-of-the-money naked options. (But they might discover that collecting pennies in front of a steam roller is steady money for a while, until they trip…) And sometimes, like the proverbial frog swimming in a slowly heating pot, they follow their strategy with iron discipline and refuse to jump out until their account has boiled away.

In a nutshell, although winning is easy, losing is hard – very hard! Unfortunately, *every* strategy has losing periods. Therefore, a successful trader must be able to handle losing. There is always uncertainty – whatever statistics may tell you, there is a real possibility that losses will continue and your account will be wiped out. Living with that degree of uncertainty, and making good decisions under the pressure of large drawdowns, is beyond most people. Even those who can handle it might find it unappealing. The image of the bronzed trader, casually chalking up large profits working for an hour in the morning before hitting the beach, just isn't reality. Too often, that leisure time turns to ashes if the morning's trades haven't worked.

The happiest traders use other people's money! Those wunderkinds in bank trading rooms, earning mega-salaries, have an absolute ball because, when push comes to shove, *they are not under the gun.* You would be very surprised how many of those superstars fail when they go solo. Carefree, objective decision making gives way to stressed, fearful, emotional, reactive actions, and decision quality plummets. Fear and hope triumph over calm and reason every time.

Psychology. Be in no doubt that it's the key to trading success. Don't ask me how to change your make up – I don't know. Maybe you have to be born that way. Maybe some people are just more comfortable with risk, uncertainty and volatility than others.

Things are always going wrong for traders; there are plenty of opportunities to think "if only I'd done *that*!", but if you are the sort of person who obsesses over things, broods about what might have been and can't let it go, then stick to a normal job – trading isn't for you. Traders live from transaction to transaction. When one goes wrong, they pick themselves up, brush themselves off and enter the next transaction without regret. They don't beat themselves up. Critically, they don't lose confidence. They learn from failure, but they don't berate themselves for it; they forgive themselves!

One thing you can do to help yourself is "wear clothes that suit you". Trading comes in a huge number of styles and flavours; make sure you choose one that matches you perfectly. I'm an impatient fellow who likes quick results, and I don't sleep well with open positions in volatile markets. I like to know where I stand before I go to play. I'm paranoid about holding open positions when markets are closed or in low volume out-of-hours sessions. I'm fearful of violent market moves that I can't react to instantly. So, I day trade. At the end of each and every day, I know my situation and I have no open positions to worry about while the market is closed.

I don't mind a losing day. I find the certainty that I have taken a loss today easier to handle than the uncertainty of being in an open position which might leave me exposed to unexpected market moves. Other traders are different. Maybe they prefer longer-term trades, with lower trading costs and potentially larger profits. Maybe they abhor leverage. Or maybe they need to have absolute control over their risk exposure by using option strategies. Whatever floats your boat – the key thing is to marry your strategy to your personality. Choose a style that makes you comfortable and doesn't keep you awake at night. If you find something that works for you, stick with it like you would with an old pair of comfortable slippers. Your trading style should lower your stress levels, not elevate them!

BIBLIOGRAPHY

I list below some books that have influenced me and that I would recommend to others.

The Trading Game by Ryan Jones (John Wiley & Sons), 1999

Techniques Of Tape Reading by Vadym Graifer and Chris Schumacher (McGraw-Hill Professional), 2003

The Disciplined Trader by Mark Douglas (NYIF), 1990

Beyond Candlesticks by Steve Nison (John Wiley & Sons), 1994

Financial Freedom Through Electronic Day Trading by Van K. Tharp and Brian June (McGraw-Hill Professional), 2001

Trading for a Living by Alexander Elder (John Wiley & Sons), 1993

Market Wizards by Jack D. Schwager (Marketplace Books), 2006

Reminiscences of a Stock Operator by Edwin Lefèvre (Harriman House Definitive Editions), 2017

THANKS
FOR READING!

Our readers mean everything to us at Harriman House. As a special thank-you for buying this book let us help you save as much as possible on your next read:

If you've never ordered from us before, get £5 off your first order at **harriman-house.com** with this code: `dtgf1`

Already a customer? Get £5 off an order of £25 or more with this code: `dt25gf`

Get 7 days' FREE access to hundreds of our books at **volow.co** – simply head over and sign up.

Thanks again!
from the team at

 Harriman House

Milton Keynes UK
Ingram Content Group UK Ltd.
UKHW050155210724
445567UK00007B/3